A Discussion of the Origins of Thinking on Arms Control
The Sarajevo Fallacy

KENNETH M. JENSEN AND KIMBER M. SCHRAUB, EDITORS

UNITED STATES
INSTITUTE OF PEACE

Washington, D.C.

The United States Institute of Peace
1550 M Street, NW
Washington, District of Columbia 20005

Printed in the United States of America

First printing 1990

Library of Congress Cataloging-in-Publication Data

Discussion of the origins of thinking on arms control: the Sarajevo
fallacy / Kenneth M. Jensen and Kimber M. Schraub, editors.
        p.   cm.
    First in the monthly series of public workshops held by the United
States Institute of Peace, given on Aug. 11, 1988.
        ISBN 1-878379-02-X
    1. Nuclear arms control—History—Congresses. 2. World War,
1914–1918—Causes—Congresses. 3. Peace—History—Congresses.
I. Jensen, Kenneth M. (Kenneth Martin), 1944– . II. Schraub,
Kimber M. III. United States Institute of Peace.
JX1974.7.D65 1990   89-26870
327.1′74′09—dc20   CIP

The United States Institute of Peace

The United States Institute of Peace is an independent, nonpartisan, federal institution created and wholly funded by Congress to strengthen the nation's capacity to promote the peaceful resolution of international conflict. Established in 1984, the Institute has its origins in the tradition of American statesmanship, which seeks to limit international violence and to achieve a just peace based on freedom and human dignity. The Institute meets its congressional mandate to expand available knowledge about ways to achieve a more peaceful world through an array of programs including grantmaking, a three-tiered fellowship program, research and studies projects, development of library resources, and a variety of citizen education activities. The Institute is governed by a bipartisan, fifteen-member Board of Directors, including four *ex officio* members from the executive branch of the federal government and eleven individuals appointed from outside federal service by the President of the United States and confirmed by the Senate.

Forthcoming publications include:

The Meaning of Munich Fifty Years Later
A Look at "The End of History?"
Is it Feasible to Negotiate Chemical and Biological Weapons Control?
Approaches to Peace: An Intellectual Map
Guides to Library of Congress Subject Headings and Classification on Peace and International Conflict Resolution

Board of Directors

Contents

Preface

For many students of military conflicts, nothing proves more dramatically the need for U.S.-Soviet arms talks than the tragedy of World War I. According to a widely accepted scenario, the West blundered into one of the most destructive conflicts in history as a result of tensions generated by reckless arms build-ups and the concomitant weakening of the European security system. By 1914, the international atmosphere was so inflamed that it took just one incident—the assassination at Sarajevo of Archduke Franz Ferdinand—to bring about an unavoidable explosion. Although historians have changed their minds time and again on the details, the lesson commonly drawn from Sarajevo is that a surfeit of arms eventually leads to war. Correspondingly, arms control has been viewed as a path to peace.

Recently, however, this reliance on arms reduction has come under strong attack from a revisionist school of American scholars. In their opinon, the conventional analysis of World War I is wrong: it was men and the political intentions of their nations—not arms—that brought about the war. This interpretation brings strongly into question the widely held view that arms control in itself leads to peace.

To explore this question, the United States Institute of Peace held the first in its series of Public Workshops at the University Club in Washington, D.C., in August, 1988. The Institute gave the event the title of a stimulating article by Patrick Glynn published in the *National Interest* in the fall of 1987: "The Sarajevo Fallacy: The Historical and Intellectual Origins of the Arms Control Theology." Twenty-two distinguished panelists participated, ranging from high-level present and former policymakers to noted foreign affairs journalists to war and peace scholars. (Their biographies can be found in the Appendix of this publication.) The Institute asked each participant to read and reflect upon "The Sarajevo Fallacy," and four of the panelists to provide extensive written commentaries. Each was asked to consider the question of whether, and to what extent, "The Sarajevo Fallacy"—and the sort of thinking it represents—deepens understanding of the causes of war, deterrence, arms control, and the special problems of democracies in waging peace.

As hoped, the event proved lively and the debate contentious. Glynn opened the workshop by tracing the roots of the "Sarajevo fallacy" to turn-of-the-century liberal-democratic thinkers in the West—such as Britain's Lord Grey—who brushed off as "naive" the view, as Glynn put it, "that there are good guys and bad guys" in the international arena. If political mistakes and motivations play only a limited role in determining events, these thinkers concluded, conflicts must be caused by other forces—most frequently, the spiraling tensions arising out of arms races and defense pacts. For those sharing this way of thinking, said Glynn, "the lesson of Sarajevo seemed to be that the very efforts [the Entente] powers took to prevent war—namely, the accumulation of military power and formation of alliances—produced the opposite results." According to Glynn, this traditional analysis is fallacious: the classical liberal-democratic model of what caused the Great War is glaringly at odds with what actually happened. "In simplest terms, World War I was caused by German aggression, by British indecision, and by the weak structure of the alliance system" that Britain, France, and Russia had cobbled together.

If arms races and deterrence strategies do not cause wars, said Glynn, it follows that arms talks and attempts at disarmament are not as useful as we would like to believe. "The debates that go on in Congress, year after year, about this or that weapons system being destabilizing and creating tensions, are rooted in an intellectual fallacy," Glynn argued. "The MX missile will not cause a World War III any more than the dreadnought was a contributing cause to World War I.... Arms control was tried on a major scale before [both] World War I and World War II, but it did not succeed in stemming the German build-up; it only made things worse."

The participants tended to agree with Glynn regarding the origins of World War I; few, however, were willing to concede Glynn's point that the current thinking about the need for arms control rests so squarely on the Sarajevo fallacy. Following the lead of the *New Republic*'s Leon Wieseltier, all agreed that some arms control was surely useful: "Elimination of certain weapons systems would [surely] eliminate certain [military] options."

The main cause for dispute among the participants was Glynn's implicit revival of the "good guys, bad guys" theory of international relations. Some, like Charles Fairbanks, Jr., applauded Glynn for discarding mechanistic understandings of how wars start, but warned that such notions as deterrence and peace-through-strength were no better methods of preventing war than arms control. Others, like J. David Singer, felt that the Sarajevo example proved nothing: "The lessons of history will never be learned by looking at a single case." Singer also disputed the view that war is primarily a function of rational choice by politicians— good or bad. He cited research showing that disputes that take place in the context of arms races are "three times more likely to lead to war" than conflicts that develop in less contentious times.

Several participants agreed with Michael Mandelbaum that there was a substantial difference between the era of the two world wars and the nuclear era. In 1914 and in 1939, the Germans could calculate that their war gains would outweigh their losses, and on that basis, could opt for military solutions. Nobody can make similar calculations in the nuclear age, according to Mandelbaum, and "that makes arms control a much more serious and rational proposition" than it was before.

Although in responding to such comments Glynn eventually agreed that some arms control may be relevant to preventing war in our time, he cautioned that successful arms control was possible only if there is "a fundamental change in the nature of Soviet policy and culture." In dealing with such adversaries, liberal democracies must break their peculiar habit of pursuing "half-Hawk, half-Dove policies"—that is, half-arms control and half-deterrence policies: "It's...these mixed policies that democracies pursue as a compromise...between common sense and the Sarajevo fallacy that can get them into trouble, precisely because [such policies] present an ambiguous face to an opponent and can be exploited."

These paragraphs provide but a taste of the full discussion at the Public Workshop. In this compilation the reader will find virtually the entire range of basic arms control issues raised and debated, and some significant history revisited and reevaluated. Included is the article by Patrick Glynn, on which the commentators and panelists reflected prior to participating; Glynn's opening remarks and the written comments of Leon Wieseltier, Charles Fairbanks, Jr., J. David Singer, and Harry Summers, Jr.; a brief rejoinder from Glynn; and an edited transcription of the general discussion that ensued thereafter. Glynn's article appears with the permission of the *National Interest*.

Samuel W. Lewis
President
United States Institute of Peace

PART I

Patrick Glynn Defines the "Sarajevo Fallacy"

PATRICK GLYNN*

The Sarajevo Fallacy:
The Historical and Intellectual
Origins of Arms Control Theology

In our time, the hope for peace and the fear of war converge on the phenomenon of the arms race. At the root of this hope and fear lies the widely shared conviction that the arms race itself is inherently dangerous and ultimately destabilizing. So firmly established is this belief in our political discourse that, forty years after the dawn of the nuclear era, we have ceased to wonder whence it came.

As a result of this conviction, Western strategy today remains torn between two fundamentally opposing premises: the notion that strength deters aggression, and the competing belief that the arms race itself may be a cause of war. Over the past forty years, the view that the arms race could lead to catastrophe has continually challenged and unsettled the Western faith in nuclear deterrence. However successful we may have been in guaranteeing peace through our military strength, we have been wary of the means at our disposal. We have been haunted by the fear that the very measures we take to secure our safety could be driving us to oblivion.

Hence, in large measure, the intense Western preoccupation with arms control. Much of the urgency with which we have pursued arms control over the past three decades stems from the

*Patrick Glynn's article originally appeared in the *National Interest*, No. 9 (Fall 1987): 3–32. The United States Institute of Peace has been granted permission to reprint the article in full.

assumption that arms races are indeed a cause of war. This conception helped propel arms control to the center of America's national security agenda in the 1960s, setting the stage for the Strategic Arms Limitation Talks (SALT).

At issue here is a rarely challenged set of assumptions about international relations that together define a powerful orthodoxy among the Western foreign policy elite: the belief that arms races spring from an "action-reaction phenomenon"; that the action-reaction pattern is inherently destabilizing and produces mounting tensions; and that finally, war, if it comes, is likely to arise "accidentally" in this climate of heightened suspicion, as a result of critical "misperceptions" during a crisis.

As it happens, all these conceptions predate SALT and even the nuclear age. They have a specific historical origin: in revisionist interpretations of the Sarajevo crisis of July 1914, the crisis that led to the outbreak of World War I. It was the popular understanding of the origins of World War I, not the atomic bomb or the Cold War and the balance of terror, that laid the basic theoretical foundations of modern arms control thinking. The real dividing line in modern reflection on the causes of war is not 1945 but 1919.

The revisionist interpretation of World War I gave birth to two fundamentally novel conceptions: first, that major wars could occur by "accident"; and second, that arms races could cause them. The latter view was not entirely without precedent. Advocacy of disarmament began to be a factor in British politics as early as the mid-nineteenth century, and even before World War I British radicals opposing rearmament had spoken generally of armaments as a "threat to peace." It was only after that war, however, that the arms race thesis became codified, and disarmament and arms control measures began to be thought of as the fundamental method of preserving peace.

The classical statement of the arms race thesis, one that echoed an increasingly widespread view, was offered in 1925 by Edward Grey, who spoke with particular authority, having been Britain's foreign secretary at the outbreak of World War I:

> The moral is obvious; it is that great armaments lead inevitably to war. If there are armaments on one side, there must be armaments

on other sides.... Each measure taken by one nation is noted, and leads to counter-measures taken by others.... Fear begets suspicion and distrust and evil imaginings of all sorts, till...every government regards every precaution of every other Government as evidence of hostile intent....

The enormous growth of armaments in Europe, the sense of insecurity and fear caused by them—it was these that made war inevitable. This, it seems to me, is the truest reading of history and the lesson that the present should be learning from the past, in the interests of future peace, the warning to be handed on to those who come after us.[1]

Conceptions such as these decisively shaped the British (and for that matter the American and French) approach to security problems for the two decades following World War I, producing the disastrous disarmament movement of the interwar decades—that movement which, as Walter Lippman said, tragically succeeded in disarming those nations that wished to disarm. These ideas were largely responsible for the debacle in Munich.

Today the vision of Sarajevo on which Grey and the Munich generation based their political vision persists in both explicit and implicit forms.

At the explicit level, the Sarajevo crisis is often cited as the counterexample to Munich. From the Munich episode we learn that weakness and appeasement tempt aggression; from the Sarajevo crisis, we are said to learn that vigilance and careful military preparations, even for apparently defensive purposes, may likewise lead to war. Henry Kissinger is one notable subscriber to this view. As he wrote in *Years of Upheaval*,

Our age must learn the lessons of World War II, brought about when the democracies failed to understand the designs of a totalitarian aggressor.... But we must remember as well the lesson of World War I, when Europe, *despite* the existence of a military balance, drifted into a war no one wanted and a catastrophe that no one could have imagined. Military planning drove decisions; bluster and posturing drove diplomacy. Leaders committed the cardinal sin of statecraft: They lost control over events.

At the implicit level, the lesson of Sarajevo has become codified in a substantial body of academic theory about arms races and international politics: among the earliest examples, the influential work of Ole R. Holsti and Robert C. North on "accidental war" in the mid-1960s; among the most recent, the work of such scholars as Jack Snyder and Stephen Van Evera on the so-called "cult of the offensive." The latter research, summarized in a recent issue of *International Security* entirely devoted to analyzing the events of July 1914, provides, in effect, a more sophisticated statement of the basic proposition that arms races cause wars.[2]

It is worth noting that the revisionist interpretation of Sarajevo also had a critical effect on a pivotal event in post-war American history. In their response to the Cuban missile crisis, President Kennedy and his advisors were decisively influenced by Barbara Tuchman's prize-winning book on the origins of World War I, *The Guns of August*—essentially a popularization of the revisionist thesis. After Soviet missiles were discovered in Cuba, the president told his advisors that he did not wish subsequent generations to read a book titled "The Missiles of October." The "arms control" project itself, spurred by the Cuban missile crisis and spearheaded by Robert S. McNamara, the advisor most influential in shaping the U.S. response to that episode, was conceived in no small measure as an effort to avoid future nuclear "Sarajevos."

What is astonishing is that at the very time when it was beginning to exert a major influence on America's security policy, this interpretation of Sarajevo was being decisively refuted. In 1961, a year before Tuchman's volume captured the imagination of Kennedy's Camelot, the West German historian Fritz Fischer published a painstakingly researched volume which called into radical doubt the whole conventional wisdom about the July 1914 crisis. Using extensive documentary evidence, Fischer showed that German leaders consciously resolved to risk a "preventive war," and did so knowing that a full-scale Continental war might result. Thus, far from being unforeseen or "accidental," World War I was the product of a deliberate bid by the German leadership for European domination.[3]

Initially, Fischer's book excited enormous controversy. Yet even by the mid-1960s, the work of the Fischer school had revolutionized the historiography of World War I, in West

Germany and indeed the West as a whole. Though other historians have since added qualifications and refinements to Fischer's thesis, and some ancillary elements of his case remain in dispute, the main lines of Fischer's argument have survived extensive scholarly scrutiny and been confirmed.

Vindication of the Fischer thesis should not have been surprising. The "revisionist" version of the war's origins had arisen during the 1920s and 1930s in response more to contemporary political factors than to any hunger for objective historical scholarship. Eager to free herself of the charge that she was responsible for the war—a charge which legitimated the onerous reparations demanded by the Versailles Treaty—Germany mounted a massive propaganda campaign involving extensive (though selective) publications of state documents. In an effort to discredit the overthrown Russian monarchy, the newly installed Bolshevik regime in Moscow likewise began to release selected archival publications. These documents seemed to shift blame away from Germany—a tendency abetted by appeasement-minded politicians in the West like David Lloyd George, who for political reasons in the 1930s declared that the great powers had "slithered" into war in 1914. Under these influences, historians, especially in America and Britain, increasingly began to play down German responsibility, shifting blame more and more to impersonal factors such as militarism, nationalism, and the arms race itself. This view in turn became deeply ingrained in Western thinking about war and peace.

By rights, the findings of the Fischer school should have prompted a radical reevaluation of our entire thinking about the problem of arms races and "accidental" war. Fischer's evidence implicitly challenged a host of orthodox assumptions about international politics. Such a rethinking, however has been slow to occur. In 1973, the Australian historian Geoffrey Blainey noted in his fine volume *The Causes of Wars* that Fischer's evidence essentially invalidated the traditional claims either that World War I was "accidental" or that it was caused by the arms race. But remarkably enough, apart from Blainey's critical review of the Sarajevo paradigm, and one recent article in *Commentary* which points out some of the implications of Fischer's basic findings, policy discussion for more than two decades has failed to absorb, or even to register, the implications of the Fischer thesis.[4] This failure is extraordinary, and important. For as it turns out, the Sarajevo crisis and the period leading up to it teach a lesson quite different from what it has conventionally been thought to teach—a lesson about arms races, disarmament, crisis, and war hardly dissimilar from that taught by Munich itself.

In one respect the arms race thesis was accurate. Obviously there had been a vast increase in the size of national arsenals before World War I, and in every case—but perhaps most conspicuously in the Anglo-German naval competition—the increases were intensified by an ever more explicit rivalry among the various powers. "The continent," the London *Economist* complained in 1879, "has been converted into a series of gigantic armed camps, within each of which a whole nation stands in arms."

Figures on defense spending for the various nations indicate the pattern. Between 1870 and 1914, French defense spending roughly doubled, British defense spending nearly tripled, and German defense spending increased tenfold.[5] Reasons for this were several. In part, growing defense expenditures were a natural consequence of Europe's burgeoning industrial and economic might. Governments were spending more on armaments, but they were also spending more on everything else. Indeed, in every nation except Germany, non-defense spending exceeded defense spending in 1914. Technology was also a factor. With rapid technological advances, new "generations" of weaponry began to emerge, and existing weapons quickly became superannuated. This was particularly true in naval construction. Commissioned in 1906, Britain's HMS *Dreadnought*, for example, was so much bigger and faster than any warship then in service that in principle it rendered the whole of the existing British navy—and by implication, the ships of every other power—obsolescent.

Yet the expansion in military and naval forces was also fueled by explicit rivalries, especially the naval competition between Germany and Great Britain. In the years leading up to World War I, the naval programs of the two nations seemed continually to react upon one another. Britain experienced a series of naval "scares" inspired by apparent surges in the German building program, which led in turn to increases in the British naval estimates. Germany, meanwhile, responded to British technical innovations—notably the commissioning of the *Dreadnought* and subsequent increase in the displacement of ships, thickness of armor, and caliber of guns—with corresponding increases of her own. One of the major foreign policy disputes in pre-war Britain concerned the question of how to cope with this escalating arms race.

Advocates of arms control in the nuclear era have often suggested that the Anglo-German naval rivalry forms an especially close parallel to the present nuclear arms competition between the United States and the Soviet Union. In the words of a recent textbook produced by a Stanford University arms control group:

> ...The Anglo-German arms race is one of the closest historical analogues to today's U.S.-Soviet arms competition. The weapons involved were major technological systems that had never been tested. They were based on a doctrine very close to today's strategic theories. Their construction was supported by military and industrial interests on each side. And the naval race may have been one of the substantial causes of World War I.[6]

The first point here is valid: there is a close analogy. However, the lessons to be drawn from it are diametrically opposed to what this text suggests and what is usually taught.

"Moderation Breeds Moderation"

Though the phrase would not be coined by Robert S. McNamara until three-quarters of a century later, the notion of an "action-reaction phenomenon" had already become central to British liberal thinking about armaments by the turn of the century. The "radical" wing of the Liberal party was convinced that the German naval build-up was basically a response to the British program. "The rapid increase in the German Navy is due more to the example set by Britain between 1895 and 1905," argued G.P. Gooch, a young radical writer who later became famous as a historian of World War I, "than to any other cause...." Since, in the words of another radical commentator, the "Germans were merely following the lead of British naval policy," the radicals argued that self-restraint and concessions on Britain's part would produce corresponding self-restraint and concessions on the part of Germany. This conviction was summarized by the radicals' slogan, "moderation breeds moderation."[7]

On the German side, meanwhile, signals were mixed. At times, Germany appeared eager to show off her growing naval capability—as when the Kaiser exhibited virtually the full German fleet in Kiel Bay for his visiting uncle, Edward VII of England, in 1904. On other occasions German officials seemed eager to play it down. In 1907, for example, Admiral von Tirpitz, the Reich marine secretary and architect of the German naval program, denied before the Reichstag either that the German navy was designed to threaten Britain or that Germany had any intention of challenging British naval hegemony—denials later repeated by the Kaiser himself.

As it turns out, however, British efforts at "moderation" failed to bring German moderation in return. The pre-war period witnessed a series of British disarmament initiatives, none of which met with success. One of the ironies of August 1914 is that England entered the war under a Liberal government which had come to office in 1905 ambitious for international disarmament.

The first major British attempt to achieve understanding with Germany occurred in the months preceding the Second Hague Conference on disarmament in 1907. (An earlier Hague Conference in 1899 had failed to yield any disarmament measures.) The radical wing of the Liberal party pressed the cabinet to formulate concrete disarmament proposals. "England as the predominant naval power," argued one radical magazine, "could well afford to take the initiative in such negotiations, and the present Government will not fulfil the expectations of its supporters if it fails to do so." Though the government was split between the "radical" or pacifist wing and "imperialist" wing of the party, disarmament remained a central plank of the Liberal platform and a key to finding money for the Liberal party's ambitious new programs of social reform.

At the prodding of the Liberal cabinet, the Admiralty agreed to a 25 percent reduction in Britain's 1906–07 naval estimates, including slowdowns in the planned production schedule for large battleships or "dreadnoughts," destroyers, and submarines. Dreadnought production was reduced from four to three, and then, under further pressure from the radicals, to two. The government presented the cuts as an explicit stimulus to the disarmament negotiations at the Hague. "We desire to stop this rivalry," the prime minister, Campbell-Bannerman, told the Commons in 1906, "and to set an example in stopping it."

The German reception was less than cordial. In conversations with Edward VII during the English king's visit to Germany in 1906, William II referred to the Hague disarmament talks as "humbug." Convinced by the German response that general disarmament talks would fail, Grey proposed some mutual exchanges of information on projected arms increases—in effect, what we now call "confidence-building measures." These, too, were rejected by the Germans. In April 1907 Prince von Bülow, the German chancellor, ruled out German participation in disarmament discussions at the Hague. "We confine ourselves," he said, "to allowing those Powers which look forward to some result from that discussion to conduct the discussion alone." The remark was greeted with laughter and cheers in the Reichstag.

It is true that the reductions proposed by the government involved no serious risk to British national security. The Liberal cabinet was forced to claim as much when proposing the gesture. Balfour, the Conservative leader and an opponent of disarmament, noted the inconsistency of offering to foreign governments as a concession what the government argued at home would have no ill effects. Moreover, the Liberal concessions coincided with a significant qualitative improvement in the navy. It was partly the technological edge the *Dreadnought* gave Britain that persuaded the Admiralty to consent to the government's scheme of cutting the naval budget.

Nonetheless, there is little question regarding the sincerity of the Liberal cabinet's hopes that this gesture would provide at least the initial impetus to the disarmament process. Unilateral reductions on this scale were, after all, completely unprecedented. As Grey explained to the French ambassador Paul Cambon: "Great Britain had sometimes been held up to other Parliaments as the nation which was forcing the pace and necessitating expenditure. Now we are anxious to make it clear that we were not forcing the pace, and to get this recognized, in the hope that public opinion abroad would discourage increased [armaments] expenditure by other governments." The foreign secretary told the Commons: "I do not believe that at any time has the conscious public opinion in the various countries of Europe set more strongly in the direction of peace than at the present time, and yet the burden of military and naval expenditure goes on increasing. We are all waiting on each other."

Yet not only did the British initiatives fail to produce results, but the Foreign Office senior clerk, Eyre Crowe, wrote in 1907 that British disarmament efforts were actually *stimulating* the German build-up: "Our disarmament crusade has been the best advertisement of the German Navy League and every German has now been persuaded that England is exhausted, has reached the end of her tether, and must speedily collapse, if the pressure is kept up." At the end of 1907, Tirpitz submitted a supplemental navy bill, providing for a new, previously unscheduled acceleration in the pace of the German build-up.

However, concerned at the effects of their posture on British opinion, the Germans soon thereafter launched a "peace offensive"—a public relations campaign specifically designed to assuage British feeling and prevent a mobilization of English opinion in favor of further arms increases. The Kaiser visited England to reassure the British concerning German naval plans. Early the following year, he went so far as to write a lengthy personal letter to the British First Lord of the Admiralty. "It is absolutely nonsensical and untrue," he remonstrated, "that the German Navy Bill is to provide a Navy meant as a 'Challenge to British Naval Supremacy.' The German fleet is built against nobody at all. It is solely built for Germany's needs in relation with that country's rapidly growing trade." The Kaiser objected strenuously that the German navy was being used in Britain to stir up public opinion against Germany. Metternich, Berlin's ambassador to London, was instructed to reassure the British at every opportunity of the benign character of Germany's intentions.

These protestations of innocence were, to put it mildly, less than sincere. In 1907 it was easy for British liberal opinion to suppose that Germany was merely responding to British naval initiatives; after all, Britain was at that time far ahead, boasting a fleet of forty-seven capital ships plus the *Dreadnought* to Germany's twenty-one. But when Germany accelerated her naval program in 1906 and 1907, she was not, as British disarmament advocates argued, merely responding to British example but actually carrying out a program that had been set down a decade earlier. The reason that British "moderation " failed to inspire reciprocal German self-restraint was essentially that radical opinion had misdiagnosed the motive at the basis of the arms race.

At the basis of the German building effort was an explicit and carefully calculated plan to challenge British naval supremacy, which had been spelled out as early as 1897 in a secret memorandum from Tirpitz to the Kaiser:

> For Germany the most dangerous naval enemy at the present time is England. It is also the enemy against which we most urgently require a certain measure of naval force as a political power factor.... Our fleet must be so constructed that it can unfold its greatest military potential between Heligoland and the Thames.

The navy was thus envisioned from the beginning as a "political power factor" to be used against Britain; the whole naval effort posited Britain as *the* enemy. Germany, Tirpitz said, should concentrate its "efforts on the creation of a battle-fleet against England which alone will give us maritime influence vis-à-vis England." Over the long run, Tirpitz planned nothing less than to create a German fleet that, if necessary, could defeat the Royal Navy at sea. "'Victorious' is the decisive word," Tirpitz noted in the margins of a secret document, "hence let us concentrate our resources on this victory."[8]

Analysts in the Reich Navy Office predicted that with a rapid building program executed over twenty years' time, Germany could produce a navy two-thirds the size of Britain's—a ratio that strategists of the day argued was adequate to defeat a naval enemy. The difference in size would be compensated for, Tirpitz argued, by better training, organization, and leadership, and by more modern equipment. This would permit Germany, already Europe's leading land power, to transform herself into at least a practical equal of the world's supreme naval force. The plan, the historian V.R. Berghahn writes, was "with the help of the Navy...to overthrow the status quo internationally."

It should be stressed that the German strategy was primarily political. The point was not to launch a surprise attack on Britain; the 2:3 ratio by 1920 that was envisioned—and that was the best that the German economy could sustain given its other commitments—would never have permitted that. The idea instead was to stalemate British naval power—to create a balance such that the Royal Navy, if drawn into a battle, could be defeated by the German force. Having sustained vast losses at the hands of Germany, Tirpitz reasoned, the British navy would then be at the mercy of the French and Russian fleets. With British naval supremacy canceled and Britain unable to risk attack, she would have no choice but to take German demands on the international stage more seriously. Such was the detailed rationale behind Tirpitz's famous "risk theory." With a navy so powerful Germany could, as the admiral put it, "expect 'fair play' from England." "Keep building," went the refrain in the Reich Navy Office, "until they come to us." For all his public protestations to the contrary, William was accustomed to refer to the navy, in the privacy of the German court, as his "Flotte gegen England," his "navy against England."

Liberal efforts to end or slow the arms race thus failed to take into account the political motivation at the basis of the rivalry: the German desire to transform the international status quo. As Crowe noted in a Foreign Office memorandum of 1910: "The building of the German fleet is but one of the symptoms of the disease. It is the political ambitions of the German government and nation which are the source of the mischief."

The fundamental character of Germany's challenge to Britain should be understood. Mutual suspicion of a general sort between sovereign states might have led to continual competition in arms between Germany and Britain resembling the naval competition between Britain and France, or Britain and Russia, at the turn of the century. But for the most part Britain, France, and Russia were building their navies to *preserve* the European balance of power; Germany, by contrast, began arming in order to change it. The hegemonic political ambitions of Germany, directed first toward colonial possessions but later toward the Continent itself, endowed the Anglo-German competition with a special intensity, transforming a generalized rivalry into an all-out arms race. The arms race was merely the outward manifestation of the fundamental incompatibility between the political aims of the two powers. Britain sought, one could say of necessity, to preserve her naval superiority; Germany sought to overthrow it.

Notably, had German ambitions been fully acknowledged, they would not have proved acceptable even to the most pacifist sectors of British opinion. Most radicals understood well enough that for Britain, an island power, naval supremacy was a life-and-death matter. For one thing, the practical alternative to defending Britain with superior naval strength was a large army, which implied the institution of national conscription; investment in the navy was thus from a certain perspective an anti-militarist measure for the British, reducing the need for a large military influence in British domestic life. But beyond that, the strength of the navy affected Britain's safety—her commerce and even her supply of food—in a way that would never be true in the German case. Winston Churchill angered many Germans but was basically correct when he argued in 1911 that the German navy was to Germany "in the nature of luxury": "Our naval power involves British existence. It is existence to us; it is expansion to them...."

The radical agitation for disarmament was inspired not by any acceptance of German ambitions but rather by a denial of their existence—a failure to acknowledge the fundamental political dimension of the problem. Liberal opinion assumed that once the arms rivalry itself was diffused, Germany would be content to coexist on terms compatible with the status quo. This assumption followed naturally from the widespread liberal belief that it was Britain, not Germany, that was "forcing the pace."

German strategy, in turn, depended upon keeping German strategic intentions concealed. By comparison with more modern regimes, the government of Wilhelmine Germany demonstrated notable ineptitude in this respect. The Kaiser, whom Kiderlen, the German secretary of state, referred to privately as "William the Sudden," did not count public relations among his strong suits. Nonetheless, German leaders knew success demanded that the British government not be alerted to the full extent of German plans and, more important, that British public opinion not be aroused to any significant degree by the German threat. "The English," the Kaiser affirmed, "must get used to the German fleet. And from time to time we must assure them that the fleet is not built against them." Or as Bülow, reiterating Tirpitz's "risk theory," asked in 1909, "How can we get through the dangerous zone which we have to traverse until we are so strong at sea that in attacking us England would run a risk out of all proportion to any probable result?" He proposed a consistent foreign policy "without rhodomontade or provocation" designed to lull British statesmen into acceptance of a gradual shift in the status quo.

Yet as regards British recognition of Germany's long-term strategic intentions, the Germans had perhaps less immediately to fear than they sometimes believed. The German leadership thought in terms of the long run; the British in this period were not on the whole accustomed to think in terms of grand strategy, even about the naval question. By the second Navy Law or "Novelle" of 1900, Tirpitz had arranged things so that the Reichstag was voting to approve naval expenditures for projected six-year periods. This political maneuver had the effect of insulating the naval build-up from the vicissitudes of democracy. (The Reichstag was thus not in a position to reciprocate yearly British gestures of "moderation" even had it wished to, which it did not.) Thus the German "procurement cycle," to use a modern term, was established at six years, while the overall navy strategy was designed to unfold over a span of two decades.

The British Admiralty of course also planned for the future, but in general the British political system approached naval appropriations empirically, on a year-by-year basis. By the early twentieth century, as E.L. Woodward notes, the "Naval Defense Act of 1899 was almost forgotten" and the British public "remained unfamiliar with any long-range plan of naval construction." The British calibrated yearly expenditures in light of the immediate plans and naval strengths of the other powers. Not surprisingly, the British assumed that the Germans would respond to the environment the way they themselves did: i.e., if immediate tensions could be reduced, motives for the German build-up would diminish.

If the British public tended to engage in what we now call "mirror-imaging," interpreting German conduct in terms of British psychology, so, in different ways, did the German public and the German leadership. Judging British intentions in light of their own, German officials tended to put the most sinister construction on even the most conciliatory British actions. Thus British disarmament proposals received an entirely cynical reading from Marschall, Germany's delegate at the Hague, who derided the English appeals to "freedom, humanity, civilization" as "catchwords."

From the German viewpoint, professions of goodwill by the British may have been genuine enough, but they were beside the point. They did not alter the fundamental fact of German strategic disadvantage vis-à-vis British naval power. When Philip Dumas, Britain's naval attaché in Berlin, assured Tirpitz in 1906 that British disarmament initiatives were entirely sincere, the latter offered this revealing response:

> Yes, perhaps it is true; but our people do not and will never understand such a scheme. I myself realize the Puritan form of thought such as is possessed by [Prime Minister] Sir Henry Campbell-Bannerman, and that he is perfectly honest and feels [disarmament] is a religious duty; but look at the facts. Here is England, already more than four times as strong as Germany, in alliance with Japan, and probably so with France, and you, the colossus, come and ask Germany, the pigmy, to disarm. From the point of view of the public it is laughable and Machiavellian, and we shall never agree to anything of the sort.... We have decided to possess a fleet, and that fleet I propose to build and keep strictly to my programme.

What is remarkable are the clear-headedness and political sophistication of the marine secretary's response. Tirpitz himself plainly
did not doubt British sincerity. In contrast to the German public,
roused to wholly implausible fears of a British "invasion" and
inured to the myth of Albion's perfidy by official and unofficial
navalist propaganda, Tirpitz and his colleagues in the Reich Navy
Office understood the peaceful intentions of the British Liberal
cabinet. (Unlike much of the populace, German naval officials had
no fear of a British invasion, partly because the British lacked the
army to pose such a threat. Bismarck had once remarked that if
English troops ever landed on German soil, he would have the
police arrest them.) There was a grain of truth in Tirpitz's appeal
to the intransigence of German public opinion. But at bottom the
marine secretary's intimations of helplessness in the face of it were
disingenuous, since the popular fear—not to say hatred—of Britain
had at the outset been deliberately fostered by the government. It
was Tirpitz and his long-term strategy of overcoming British naval
strength, not public resistance, which ultimately stood in the way
of an end to the naval rivalry.

Germany's "Strategic Fear"

Indeed, for all the signs that Germany feared British intentions,
German officials came to grasp with remarkable clarity the pacifist
character of the Liberal British government, and insofar as possible
they maneuvered to keep the Liberals in and the Conservatives out.
In 1907, Tirpitz actually tried to moderate the German build-up
slightly so as to avoid arousing British suspicions. As one of his
closest advisers in the Reich Naval Office wrote, if the German
building tempo increased, the "Liberal cabinet in Britain will be
thrown out of office and be replaced by a Conservative one which,
even if one hopes for the best, will, by making huge investments
in the Navy, completely obliterate all our chances of catching up
with Britain's maritime power within a measurable space of time."
When the British naval "scare" of 1909 appeared to be getting out
of hand, Bülow drew the picture for the Kaiser: "A conservative
government in England would represent a very real danger for us...."

[W]e should do all in our power to keep the Liberal party, to which all peace-loving elements in England adhere, at the helm." The whole German strategy depended upon nurturing pacifist elements in Britain to get Germany through the build-up period.

To claim that Germany was arming simply from fear of Britain, therefore, would be inaccurate. That Germany feared British power is undeniable; but it is wholly misleading to suggest that Germany was arming out of a simple sense of insecurity. A suggestion of this sort is made by the arms control textbook cited earlier:

> Because Great Britain had an empire and was an island, it had long relied heavily on its navy for defense. In 1889 it authorized construction of seventy ships, including ten battleships, over the next decade....
>
> Germany felt insecure, remembering that in 1807 England had destroyed the Danish fleet at Copenhagen by surprise. Germany moved in 1898, drawing up plans for nineteen new battleships and many lesser ships to be built over six years.

The best that can be said about his piece of conventional wisdom is that it grossly oversimplifies the evidence. It ignores the fact that Britain was sounding out Germany on the possibility of forming an alliance in 1898, the year in which the first German Navy Law was passed. True, a century earlier, the English had pre-emptively destroyed the Danish fleet in Copenhagen to prevent it from falling into Napoleon's hands and threatening Britain. This incident, wrenched from its context in the Napoleonic wars, became a staple ingredient of German navalist propaganda, and there is little question but that Germans in the early twentieth century came to fear another "Copenhagen." In 1905, for example, such fears led the Kaiser to order a partial mobilization of the German fleet and recall his ambassador from London. Yet it would be ridiculous to explain this fear as the result of a simple defensive sense of "insecurity"; it was a direct consequence of Germany's plan to alter the status quo. As Jonathan Steinberg has put it, "'Kopenhagen' really stood for a fear of what the British might do if they once found out what the Germans wanted to do."[9] The fear the government felt was a product of what Berghahn has called the "high stakes game" that the Reich was playing; it was the natural consequence of risks deliberately assumed. The "ultimate question," as Tirpitz wrote, was "either to abdicate as a world power or to take risks."

Indeed, rarely was the German government's sense of insecurity focused on British intentions. For all the talk in the Wilhelmstrasse of a "trade war" with Britain, never once did Berlin's ambassadors in London report feeling in favor of such a war. To grasp why Germany's leadership was nonetheless afraid, one must comprehend the structure of German suspicions, which were directed not so much at the *aims* as at the *power* of Germany's rivals. The fear that motivated Germany might be characterized as "strategic fear" to distinguish it from defensive or spontaneous fear per se—since it was a consequence primarily of German strategic intentions rather than of the intentions of other states. The German government feared that other powers might have the capacity to frustrate German aims, or threaten German security, if at some point in the future they formed the intention to do so. In the end, the capacity to defeat Germany was, in the eyes of the German leadership, indistinguishable in practice from the intention to do so.

Such strategic fear was in turn a consequence of the Social Darwinist cultural outlook—one might go so far as to call it an "ideology"—that pervaded both the populace and leadership in Germany at this time. Social Darwinism gained influence with elements of public opinion throughout Europe in the late nineteenth century, but nowhere else did it become so central to national thought and feeling as in Germany. The prevailing German view was that there was to be an eventual struggle for survival among states in which the Reich would either triumph or fall. The possibility of war with Britain was thus on German minds from the turn of the century onward. The tendency was to see Germany as a young state, as it were, "on the make," and to envision Britain, by contrast, as an exhausted and effeminate power in imperial decline. Germany, wrote Tirpitz in 1879, was prompting reactions among other European powers similar to "Society's responses to a social climber." "Old empires are fading away," the Kaiser affirmed in 1899, "and new ones about to be formed." Coexistence with other nations was merely a transitional phase as history progressed toward the final struggle.

Given German paranoia, it was natural enough for liberal circles in Britain to seek to allay German fears by proposing gestures of conciliation on armaments. Yet efforts to win German trust with unilateral concessions proved to be misdirected because German fears were focused on British power rather than British intentions. Far from diffusing German suspicions, such concessions tended to be ascribed, if not to treachery, then to weakness. Following what was perceived in England as one of Sir Edward Grey's more moving appeals for international disarmament before the Commons in 1911, the German naval attaché in London reported in rather typical tones to Berlin: "Grey's surrender is due to the Naval Law alone and the unshakable resolution of the German nation not to allow any diminution of this important instrument [i.e., the navy]." The British desire for disarmament was thus equated by German officials with "surrender." The Kaiser seconded his emissary's conclusion: "If we had followed the advice of Metternich and Bülow for the last four or five years and ceased to build we should now have had the 'Copenhagen' war upon us. As it is, they respect our firm resolution and surrender to the facts. So we must go on building undisturbed."

Diplomats like Metternich and Bülow urged moderation in the naval build-up for prudential reasons. But the debate among German officials concerned mainly the build-up's feasibility and risks; the goals and assumptions behind it were quite alien to the issues that occupied liberal Britain. Interestingly, opposition to Tirpitz's plan arose not when Britain offered concessions, but rather when British resolve seemed firm enough to raise doubts about the prospect of eventual German success in matching British naval strength, as eventually happened in 1912–13. Then, but only then, pragmatists like Chancellor Bethmann Hollweg were able to gain the upper hand in making their case for shifting resources away from the navy. Even so the money was not channeled, as would have been the case in Britain, into "social legislation" but rather into spending for the army—which helps explain why the

French remained nervous during the Anglo-German naval talks. The British liberal formula of reducing armaments expenditures so as to increase spending for social programs was alien to German ideology and the structure of the German regime.

Thus the action-reaction notion was accurate, if at all, only in the narrow sense that specific actions on the part of the British (e.g., the move to dreadnoughts) generally were followed by comparable steps on the part of Germany. True, Britain maintained an edge in naval technology, and Germany was in the position of following her technological lead. But this was an effect rather than a cause of the rivalry. This was not widely understood. As late as 1910 the *Economist* argued,

> The German fleet which has struck such panic is largely imaginary, and the supposed danger is entirely due to the fact that the Admiralty invented the Dreadnought and fostered the impression that this type of ship had superseded all others.... Nevertheless, spurred on by the contractors, who love these huge jobs in ironmongery, the Admiralty goes on enlarging the size of battleships.

Such arguments persisted to the very eve of the war.

Aware in general terms of a new German naval challenge by 1902, by 1906–07 the Admiralty and the Foreign Office were growing increasingly wary of German intentions and skeptical of the contention that British attempts at disarmament would curb Germany's ambition. (Notably, however, perception of a German threat did not figure into the decision to build the *Dreadnought*.) Winston Churchill, then serving in the cabinet as home secretary, later summarized the trend of those years:

> No one could run his eyes down the series of figures of British and German construction for the first three years of the liberal administration, without feeling in presence of a dangerous, if not malignant design.
>
> In 1905 Britain built 4 ships, and Germany 2.
>
> In 1906 Britain decreased her programme to 3 ships, and Germany increased her programme to 3 ships.
>
> In 1907 Britain further decreased her programme to 2 ships, and Germany further increased her programme to 4 ships.
>
> These figures are monumental.

> It was impossible to resist the conclusion, gradually forced on
> nearly every one, that if the British Navy lagged behind, the gap
> would very speedily be filled.[10]

Yet the government continued to explore methods of escaping what Campbell-Bannerman, as prime minister, had termed "the self-defeating race of armaments."

By the early twentieth century, British politics had begun to exhibit in full measure that conflict between "hawks" and "doves," which ever since has shaped disputes about the armaments programs of Western democracies. The dovish, retrenchment-minded Liberals were opposed in general by the more hawkish Tories, while the Liberal party itself was split fairly evenly between its dovish radical-pacifist and its somewhat more hawkish "imperialist" wings—a division that dated from the Boer War. British foreign policy reflected a compromise between these opposing impulses.

As late as 1908–09, Churchill himself lobbied in concert with Lloyd George for reductions in the British naval program. They seemed on the verge of getting their way, moreover, until intelligence reports from Germany revealed that Tirpitz had secretly laid down two keels ahead of the officially announced building schedule. The subsequent "panic" fundamentally altered the British outlook on Germany. Until 1909 the British had viewed France as the empire's most important potential enemy; Britain's "two-power standard" had been established with the French and Russian navies in mind. Thereafter, anxiety shifted focus to Germany.

Ironically, the alarming intelligence reports later proved to be overstated (though not, as some later claimed, manufactured by the government). Nonetheless, the extra four battleships built as a result of the 1909 panic ultimately proved crucial to British security in the opening months of the war, providing nearly the whole of the British margin of superiority in home waters in that class of vessel—a margin which Churchill, head of the Admiralty at the time of the war, later noted did not leave "much...for mischance." Churchill praised McKenna, First Lord in 1909, for resisting the cuts, noting that while Churchill and Lloyd George were "strictly right" of facts, "we were absolutely wrong in relation to the deep tides of destiny...." The exaggerated intelligence reports thus proved in the long run to serve British security.

Amid the controversy, Grey proposed more confidence-building measures, renewing the request for what we would now term "on-site inspection" of the fleets by the two countries' naval attachés.

What becomes clear is the difficulty that Britain had judging the nature and seriousness of German ambitions. As late as 1909 the cabinet remained split. In a famous memorandum dated January 1, 1907, the Foreign Office's Crowe posed the central question regarding the nature of German intentions:

> Either Germany is definitely aiming at a general political hegemony and maritime ascendancy, threatening the independence of her neighbours and ultimately the existence of England; or Germany [is] free from any such clear-cut ambition, and thinking for the present merely of using her legitimate position and influence as one of the leading Powers in the council of nations....

As Imanuel Geiss has shown, in the absence of a clear answer, Crowe advocated, in effect, a strategy of "containment," acceding to German policy as long as it remained peaceful, opposing it if it became aggressive: "So long as Germany's action does not overstep the line of legitimate protection of existing rights she can always count upon the sympathy and good-will, and even the moral support, of England...." He advised strongly against unilateral conciliation or, to use a term favored by the next generation of British statesmen, a policy of "appeasement": "That is the road paved with graceful British concessions—concessions made without any conviction either of their justice or their being set off by equivalent counterservices. The vain hopes that in this manner Germany can be 'conciliated' and made more friendly must be definitely given up." Pressure to pursue just such a concessionary policy—"moderation breeds moderation"—nonetheless persisted.

Naval talks with Germany continued intermittently up to 1914, with Grey frequently renewing his proposal for an exchange of technical information, without success. When Bethmann

Hollweg came to office as chancellor in 1909, the Germans opened a new round of negotiations. Bethmann was no believer in arms control; privately he dismissed "arms limitation between two countries who may have to defend their honor and independence against each other" as "chimerical." Nonetheless, unlike Tirpitz, he recognized that the naval race was driving Britain into closer relations with France and Russia, negating the logic of the "risk theory." Tirpitz's original hope of browbeating Britain into an alliance with Germany was beginning to appear bankrupt.

Bethmann attempted to pursue a policy that relied less on the navy per se and more on diplomacy. During negotiations from August through November 1909, the Germans offered a temporary slowdown in naval construction, but the price was high: a British promise of neutrality in any Continental war. This would have ceded to Germany at the negotiating table much of what she was seeking to gain by the naval build-up. The effect, as the British understood, would have been to shatter the Entente with France, leaving Britain isolated opposite a Continent under German domination.

Once again, the substantive problem was not so much the arms race as the underlying political cause. Germany had hegemonic ambitions; as long as she had the power, she was inclined to pursue them, whether by military or diplomatic means. The question at issue was whether Britain was willing to accede to German hegemony on the Continent. The British answer was clear enough: "[I]f we sacrifice the other Powers to Germany," Grey wrote in April 1909, "we shall eventually be attacked." Britain was willing to offer a guarantee of non-aggression and a promise of neutrality in the event of an unprovoked attack on Germany—essentially confirmation that the Entente with France was indeed purely defensive; Germany deemed such promises insufficient.

In another round of negotiations in 1912, Britain attempted to end the rivalry by offering Germany a free hand in acquiring colonial possessions. Within Germany, Bethmann's position vis-à-vis Tirpitz had been strengthened by three factors: the spiralling costs of the naval program, aggravated by continuous increases by the British in the displacement of their ships; the demands of the army for an increase in funds; and the elections of 1912, which decisively strengthened the Social Democratic minority in the Reichstag. In 1911, under pressure from the Reich Treasury, Tirpitz even began to reformulate his position, arguing that Germany might be able to achieve the "risk fleet" by way of an arms agreement with Britain which ratified the 2:3 ratio, and that in any case if negotiations failed, Germany could go on building with the aim of "enforcing" the desired ratio. Despite Tirpitz's backpedaling, however, Bethmann was still not strong enough to prevent an increase in the Reich's 1912 naval bill. When it became apparent that the new Reich navy law would require yet another matching expansion, the incentive for talks, from the British standpoint, disappeared.

"Moderation," therefore, did not breed "moderation." On the contrary, British disarmament efforts at best had no positive effect on the German resolve to build; and there is considerable evidence to suggest that the persistent British interest in disarmament stoked the fires of the German build-up by persuading German officials for a long time, not least the Kaiser himself, that their bid to challenge British power would ultimately succeed. Thus, paradoxically, the effort to achieve disarmament seems to have made an arms race all the more inevitable, while the negotiations themselves had the effect of worsening relations between the two powers by drawing attention to their irreconcilable political differences. When the German naval effort slackened, it was only because of loss of faith in the "risk theory" and financial strains within the Reich—both mainly consequences of the persistence of the British response to the German naval challenge.

In the end, it is probably fair to say that the arms negotiations failed because the underlying cause of the arms race lay beyond the power of diplomats to remedy, since it went to the very nature of German ambitions and of the German regime. In February 1914, responding to yet another campaign for British concessions by the radical wing of his own party, Grey pointed out that the arms race was "not a British matter alone" to control. "Any large increase in the building programme of any great country in Europe," he acknowledged, "has a stimulating effect upon the expenditure in other countries...." But he added that "it does not follow that a slackening in the expenditure of one country produces a diminution in the expenditure of others.... [I]t does not follow that if the leading horse slackened off, and that slackening was due to exhaustion, the effect would be a slackening on the part of others. It might be a stimulating one...." In words that still have resonance, Grey issued a caution: "[W]e must not get into the habit of thinking that if the world does not do what it seems obvious to us it ought to do, it is our fault...."

The "Minister for Slaughter"

Those who have argued that war in August 1914 came as a result of action and reaction in the arms competition have never satisfactorily explained why Britain, Germany's major competitor in the arms race and the power with the largest per capita arms expenditure in 1914, was the last nation to enter the war, and then did so only reluctantly. The arms race paradigm, at least as it comes down to us today, would seem to suggest that Britain, feeling the same suspicions and driven by the same forces as Germany, would have been equally likely to initiate the conflict. In the event, however, Britain's approach to the Sarajevo crisis was marked throughout by the greatest hesitation and reluctance. The whole British effort was directed at achieving a mediated settlement. "I hate it, I hate it!" the Austrian ambassador reported Grey as saying after the war had broken out; the British foreign secretary, the ambassador wrote to his superiors, "is in despair that his efforts to maintain the peace have gone to ruin."

Indeed, German policy in the Sarajevo crisis—her willingness to escalate the crisis by pressing Vienna to punish Serbia militarily for its alleged involvement in the Sarajevo assassination—was based in part on the belief that Britain would hold back from engagement in a Continental conflict and remain neutral.

The desire for a peaceful resolution to the crisis so manifest in London in 1914 was also apparent, in different degrees and for somewhat different reasons, in Paris and St. Petersburg—a critical fact that recent historiography has increasingly emphasized.[11] For many years, historians assumed that the predisposition to war before 1914 was roughly equal on all sides, particularly among the Continental powers. France, the revisionist argument went, was nursing a grudge over the German appropriation of Alsace-Lorraine in 1871. "For more than forty years," wrote Barbara Tuchman in *The Guns of August*, "the thought of 'Again' was the single most fundamental factor of French policy." At the same time, Russia was long suspected (erroneously) of complicity in the assassination plot. These beliefs supported the impression that the arms race was mere "action and reaction" among more or less equally ambitious and bellicose states.

Recent scholarship has called this whole picture into question. Jean-Jacques Becker's comprehensive study of French public opinion in 1914 shows that nationalism in France was much less of an influence than was long assumed. Far from coming at the culmination of a "nationalist revival," war in July 1914 took most Frenchmen utterly by surprise. Active interest in Alsace-Lorraine had for the most part died away. French nationalism itself, Raoul Giradet has written, "even if it remained obstinate in its fidelity to the lost provinces," was "no longer a conquering nationalism, a nationalism of expansion," but "a movement of defense, retreat." Only after the war was underway did France make recovery of Alsace-Lorraine her war aim. While France feared a war and prepared for the possibility of one, President Poincaré's policy remained fastidiously defensive—a policy of neither provocation nor appeasement, but of strict deterrence.

Essentially the same could be said of Russia. Defeat in the 1904–05 war with Japan had made Russian statesmen cautious, anxious to avoid policies that might lead Russia into another conflict. Among the great powers, Russia was perhaps the least affected by militarism; "turn-of-the-century Russian culture," as the historian D.C.B. Lieven has put it, "was peculiarly inhospitable to military values and virtues." More important, the strength and anti-government tenor of the left-wing parties meant that the war held within it the threat of revolution, as the conflict with Japan had shown, so that even many conservatives counseled against foreign policy risk-taking. Even Nicholas's own patriotism was balanced by a healthy fear of war, and Sazanov, the foreign minister, talked of maintaining peace so that Russia could pursue "economic reorganization" internally.

Nor were there any illusions in Berlin regarding bellicose intentions on the part of these powers. Only four months before the war broke out, Moltke, chief of the general staff in Germany, wrote to his Austrian counterpart, Conrad: "All the news which we have from Russia suggests that at present they have no intention of adopting an aggressive attitude." As for France, Moltke continued: "Even less than from Russia should we now expect an aggressive attitude from France. From a military point of view France is at present very unfavorably placed." Of the leaders of these four great powers—Germany, Britain, Russia, and France—German leaders alone were considering and discussing the possibility of a "preventive war."

With regard to the arms race itself, the direction of the action-reaction pattern is also clear: Germany was consistently the initiator. The French Chamber of Deputies voted three-year conscription only after Germany passed a massive new army bill in Germany in March 1913. The same German bill provoked the Tsar to order a large expansion of the Russian army. Nor were French and Russian anxieties unwarranted; unbeknownst to either government, German leaders at the end of 1912 had already begun to lay the groundwork for a preventive war. At a meeting of the emperor and the leading military officials on December 8, Moltke said: "I believe a war to be unavoidable and the sooner the better." Bethmann Hollweg had forwarded the army bill to the Kaiser with a note suggesting that the populace must be psychologically prepared for war.

In short, the quantities of arms accumulated before 1914 did not change the underlying characters or policies of the different regimes that amassed them. Underneath the surface of the generalized arms race, there remained a clear distinction between those powers that were wedded to the status quo and were arming defensively, and Germany, which wanted to change the balance of power radically. The fact that France and Russia increased their armies in response to Germany did not mean that their policies had altered in an aggressive direction. Similarly, the outcry of British radicals notwithstanding, the fact that Britain was spending more every year for her navy after 1907 did not mean that she was growing more aggressive; indeed, the opposite was true.

Historians who have attributed the origins of the war to impersonal forces such as modern nationalism and militarism have neglected to recognize how differently these forces acted upon the different states. George Kennan, for example, has cited as critical "the professionalization of the military, the rise of the great military bureaucracies, the growing separation of military and political thought, the abandonment of the concept of limited military operations in pursuit of limited gains."[12] While all of these generalizations clearly hold true of Germany, they do not apply with anything approaching the same force to other powers. As with discussions of nationalism, the tendency in discussing pre-war military preparations has been to enforce a false parallelism among the different states.

In fact, only in Germany did the military, in effect, conduct the foreign policy (the Kaiser himself tending to refer contemptuously to non-military Reich officials, from the chancellor on down, as "civilians"). And only in Germany did mobilization plans constrict political decisions to the point where the distinction between general mobilization and war was cast aside. Russia counted on a minimum of three to six weeks between a general mobilization order and commencement of fighting. Germany, by contrast, planned to attack and mobilize at the same time. The Schlieffen plan, which formed the basis of German strategy in August 1914, called for an attack through Belgium on France while the Russians were still busy mobilizing. This in itself violated existing diplomatic conventions, to say nothing of incipient international law. Yet it was German planning, and German planning alone, which felt no compunction to take such conventions into account.

More recent attempts to attribute the war to a generalized "cult of the offensive" are equally misleading. True, French battle tactics emphasized the offense, or defense by means of counterattack, and from a purely military standpoint this proved a ludicrous and humanly very costly strategy. But one must keep in mind the elementary distinction between French battle tactics, which may have been "offensive," and France's political posture and foreign policy, which were manifestly defensive. Moreover, while the French general staff may have been unimaginative, it was still under firm government control. "[I]n those states whose regime was democratic and parliamentary," Pierre Renouvin reminds us, "the government, between 1900 and 1914, never stopped supervising the plans of the general staff, perhaps simply because it harbored a secret mistrust of military chiefs...on the other hand, in Germany the general staff was freer in its action and freer to yield to the temptation to profit from a superiority in armaments."[13] It may be true, as proponents of the "cult of the offensive" thesis argue, that the strategic ideas and military arrangements of the era created "incentives" for pre-emption; Germany, however, was alone in yielding to the temptation.

Indeed, most of the lessons that the revisionists applied to all the powers—the predominance of militarism, the blind chauvinism of public opinion, the rigidity of military timetables, the tendency of armaments firms to fuel the arms race—in truth pertained decisively only to Germany.

To a degree that has not generally been appreciated, the forces of "militarism"—if it can be called that—were in fact very much on the defensive in Britain in the years immediately leading up to the war. Germans who had counted on the decadence of French and British culture to undermine the Entente's will in war were surprised at the patriotic fervor that took hold in the supposedly weak democratic regimes once the war was underway. Yet this wartime experience colored the manner in which commentators later interpreted pre-war history. "[I]t is true," wrote the British socialist J.A. Hobson in 1918,

> that British militarism has come with a rush in war-time and bears the appearance of a merely temporary improvisation. But those who have more closely watched the course of politics in recent years will form a different judgement.... [I]f we look to the trend of British politics and industry in the years before the war, we shall see the same drive towards militarism that we have seen in France and Germany. For the same impelling motives were at work....

Yet these sorts of claims were wholly misleading. The Krupp firm may have played an active role in driving forward the German armaments program, but by 1914 the British government had evolved an elaborate system of bureaucratic checks and balances to keep armament procurement and finance under firm civilian control. The post-war myth that the armaments manufacturers, the so-called "merchants of death," had conspired to drive the country into the war for profit had no factual basis.[14]

While it is true in a sense that naval construction "was supported by military and industrial interests on each side," as the arms control textbook puts it, such a statement ignores the radically different balance between pro- and anti-militarist forces within each of the governments. Tirpitz had the ear of the Kaiser and consistently succeeded, until 1912, in circumventing both the "civilian" ministers and the Reichstag. His British counterpart, Admiral Fisher, reported to a civilian minister, the First Lord of the Admiralty. All three First Lords before the war—Tweedmouth, McKenna, and Churchill—successfully faced powerful anti-militarist coalitions in both Parliament and the cabinet. In a Liberal government devoted to "Peace, Retrenchment, and Reform," it was no easy task for a British cabinet minister to gain support for new military or naval initiatives. The prevailing views within the cabinet can be gathered from Lloyd George's pet name for Haldane, the war minister, whom he was fond of referring to as "the Minister for Slaughter."

What was true within the governments also held for the societies as a whole. Public opinion in Britain was obviously capable of being aroused by the German threat, as occurred in the naval panic of 1909. Clearly there was a nationalist minority in Britain as in France, some jingoistic newspapers, and a nationalist literature represented most conspicuously by Kipling. But in the early twentieth century such influences were on the wane. As the Liberal landslide of 1905 itself suggests, nationalist feeling was more than counterbalanced both within and without the government by pacifist forces. And notably, while both Britain and Germany had industry-financed "Navy Leagues" which pressed for naval expansion, the organizations existed on wholly different scales within the two countries. "In 1901," notes Jonathan Steinberg, "the German *Flottenverein* had 600,000 members and associates. The Navy League in Britain had 15,000 members and an annual expenditure of under £4,000. The colossal difference in scale of the two organizations underlies the contrast between the role of the Navy in the two societies. In Germany navalism was virtually a mass movement of its own." In fact, the *Flottenverein* was the largest private organization in Germany.

Far from promoting a dangerous convergence, domestic politics pulled the two coalitions in different directions. In the Entente, public opinion acted as often as not as a brake on policy; in Germany, by contrast, the structure of domestic policies not only permitted but virtually necessitated expansionist or hegemonic policies abroad. Since the time of Bismarck, the leitmotif of German foreign policy had been "export of the social question," the effort, in Friederich von Holstein's phrase, "to divert the internal struggle to the *foreign sphere*." "Only a successful foreign policy," wrote Bülow in 1897, "can help to reconcile, pacify, rally, unify." For the ruling elites foreign expansion, success abroad, was a "method of democratic control."[15]

The key to the difference between the two nations lay in the fundamentally contrasting nature of their political regimes. By the close of the nineteenth century, Britain had become, in essence, a liberal democracy. There was a powerful middle class, the economy was largely independent of the state, and British political life was marked by a measure of freedom and tolerance simply unknown in Germany. The aristocracy had ceded control. Not that Britain was unshaken by domestic struggle. In the years leading up to World War I, civil war loomed as a possibility in Ireland, and class struggle had risen to a fevered crescendo. The violence of suffragettes, the militancy of the trade unions, and the restive mood in the army all threatened domestic tranquility. Yet, if anything, these developments distracted from rather than promoted the formation of a firm line in foreign policy.

The German situation was quite different. In the latter half of the nineteenth century, Germany underwent an extremely rapid and successful industrial revolution, but economic transformation was unaccompanied by political movement toward genuine democracy. On the contrary, authoritarian forces within German society strove to assure that the emergence of capitalism strengthened their hand. Economic modernization, largely spearheaded by the state, was pursued in the name of state grandeur; key sectors of the economy remained under direct state control. The middle class lacked access to power, while the aristocracy, imbued with a strong militarist tradition, staunchly resisted political change. Industrialization proceeded under an alliance between the agrarian aristocracy and the industrialists, between "blood and iron." It is true that the parliamentary strength of the Social Democrats grew. But this only increased the impetus for militarist agitation, since nationalism was used by Germany's authoritarian government to contain the influence of the Left. The Reichstag, its sole prerogative a veto over government spending, provided more the trappings than the substance of democratic rule.

In contrast to England, moreover, Germany retained a huge peasant class, fertile ground for nationalist agitation on the part of the aristocracy. In this freshly unified country, plagued by conflicts among classes and ethnic groups, nationalism became the social cement of the regime, while the success of *Weltpolitik* constituted the greatest proof that the Reich itself was a viable political entity.

Together these developments added up to a kind of geological shift in the European political landscape. Nineteenth century diplomacy had been preoccupied with the struggle between revolution and monarchy, between the threat represented by Napoleonic France and the conservatism represented by the Holy Alliance. Toward the end of the century this conflict began to give way to a new opposition, between the emergent liberal democracies and more authoritarian regimes—by the lights of liberalism, essentially atavistic states. In actuality, the new authoritarian states of the twentieth-century, as the heir of Europe's old monarchies, were to represent a volatile mix of the old and the new—combining modern economic power and in some measure modern political ideologies (pre-war Social Darwinism, post-war Nazism and Communism) with the traditional realpolitik perspective of the old monarchies. The modern authoritarian regime, lacking the popular legitimacy of the democracies, would be dependent for its very survival on successes in foreign affairs. The confrontation between liberal Britain and Wilhelmine Germany already exhibited many essential features of the overmastering conflict that would preoccupy nations for the remainder of the century—the struggle between democratic and totalitarian states.

"Unintentional" War

In the decade following the war, the question of differences among political regimes—an issue to which liberal thinking about international politics was never sensitive—became caught up in the related, though somewhat distinct, issue of moral responsibility for the war. The growing reluctance to dwell on the nature of "Prussian militarism" after 1919 was partly due to British and American uneasiness over the Versailles Treaty, branded by John Maynard Keynes a "Carthaginian Peace."

Nonetheless, in rejecting, on grounds of its moralistic overtones, the proposition that "Prussian militarism" was a force endemic to a certain form of government, liberal commentators sacrificed a good deal of practical insight into how the war had begun. One legacy of this oversimplification has been the fallacious notion of "unintentional" or "accidental" war—an idea that gained increasing currency during the early 1960s and became "scientifically" codified in the 1965 research of Ole R. Holsti and Robert C. North. Taking Sarajevo as their model, the two Stanford University researchers exhaustively scrutinized a selection of the state documents of the major powers from June 28 to August 1, identifying over five thousand discrete "perceptions." By devising various ratios to quantify the psychological relationship between what they termed "units of hostility" and "units of friendship," the researchers thought they had demonstrated a mathematical relationship between mounting anxieties and the escalation of the crisis. The study concluded that feelings of fear and anxiety were decisive in precipitating the war, which they implied had occurred from miscalculation, almost, as it were, inadvertently. In launching the conflict, Holsti and North contended, the Kaiser had acted irrationally, which explains why deterrence failed to deter. Indeed, the study went so far as to suggest that the "Kaiser appears to have undergone an almost complete personality change during the critical night of July 29–30." "Perceptions of inferior capability," they wrote, "will fail to deter a nation from going to war," if "perceptions of anxiety, fear, threat, or injury are great enough." However, Fischer's evidence, not yet available in English when Holsti and North wrote, simply invalidated these findings.[16]

First, it was incorrect to assume that the Germans perceived their military capabilities as "inferior." Throughout the July crisis the general staff pressed hardest for war, precisely because the generals believed the odds to be in Germany's favor. As the Bavarian ambassador in Berlin reported to his prime minister on July 31, 1914:

> In military circles here everybody is very confident. Months ago the Chief of Staff, Herr von Moltke, said that from a military point of view the moment was as opportune as it was likely to be in the foreseeable future. The reasons which he gives are:
>
> 1. The superiority of the German artillery. France and Russia have no howitzers and can therefore not fight troops in covered positions.
> 2. The superiority of the German infantry gun.
> 3. The totally inadequate training of the French troops....

Second, the Holsti-North study begged the central question that it posed: it assumed that the cause for the crisis could be discovered in the action and reaction between the powers, that the key to understanding the outbreak of war lay in understanding the immediate emotional states of national leaders. Ignored was the possibility that the escalation of the crisis to war was the product of conscious intent arrived at analytically. Such indeed was the case. "[T]he events at Sarajevo," as Imanuel Geiss has observed, "...turned out to be hardly more than a cue for the Reich to rush into action."[17] As for the Kaiser's sudden "personality change," which Holsti and North deduced from marginalia to documents dating from July 29, suffice it to say that there were manifold examples of a peculiarly vehement mode of self-expression on the part of "William the Sudden" dating from well before the Sarajevo crisis. Moreover, it cannot explain the divergence between the Kaiser and Bethmann Hollweg on July 27. After reading the humiliated Serbians' response to the Austrian ultimatum, the Kaiser wrote that Vienna had scored a "great moral victory" and added that "with it every reason for war drops away." In other words, by all appearances, the Kaiser backed away from war at the last minute. Bethmann Hollweg delayed forwarding William's comments to Vienna, and when he did, he suppressed the emperor's observation that the reasons for war were disappearing. In short, the Kaiser's emotional hesitation was overridden by the chancellor on the grounds of the latter's political calculation that Germany had already gone too far in the crisis to back down.

Recent historiography has not dealt kindly with any of the leading assumptions underpinning the conventional model of the Sarajevo crisis: the assumption that "none of the powers wanted war"; the impression that in 1914 Germany genuinely feared imminent aggression from the other powers and that she lacked confidence in her military capabilities; the belief that the Russian general mobilization on July 31 was the event that provoked the subsequent German mobilization and declaration of war.

Far from blundering into the war, German leaders were aware that they were risking general war when they deliberately prodded Austria to take military action against Serbia. The decision to give Austria carte blanche to take military action against Serbia was made during July 5–7. By July 12, Szögyény, the Austrian ambassador in Berlin, reported that "German circles that mattered" were "one might almost say urging" Austria-Hungary "to take action which might even mean military action, against Serbia." Four days earlier, after a conversation with Berlin's ambassador, the Austrian foreign minister Berchtold, told Tisza, the Hungarian prime minister, that "in Germany any deal by us with Serbia would be interpreted as a confession of weakness which must have repercussions on our position in the triple Alliance and on Germany's future policy." He added that German calculations were based on the assumption "that at present England would not participate in a war which started over a Balkan country, not even if it led to [a] clash with Russia and perhaps also with France."

On July 8 even Bethmann, always more hesitant than the generals, had already confided to his personal secretary, Kurt Riezler: "If war comes from the east so that we have to fight for Austria-Hungary and not Austria-Hungary for us we have a chance of winning. If war does not break out, if the Tsar is unwilling or France, alarmed, counsels peace, we have the prospect of splitting the Entente." The chancellor thus explicitly envisioned the possibilities not simply of a localized war involving Austria and Serbia but also of a Continental war involving Germany, Russia, and France. And while Bethmann Hollweg hoped for British neutrality, he did not totally discount the possibility that Britain would eventually join the conflict. On July 7 he told Reizler: "An action against Serbia...can lead to world war."

Given a willingness to risk a major war, the configuration of forces in the crisis was, from the German perspective, ideal: Britain would be called upon to support France and Russia over a question in which Britain had no interest, while Germany would be supporting Austria (as opposed to fickle Austria's being called upon to support Germany) in the likely event that Russia offered military support to Serbia. Popular support in Germany for a European war would be easier to assure if Russia were the enemy. Such were the advantages of a war "from the east." The key to Bethmann's strategy of localization, however, was rapid execution. In late June, European public opinion sympathized with Austria over the death of the Archduke. It was essential to his plan that Austria strike while the iron was hot, moving rapidly to exact military punishment from Serbia while still apparently angry, so that Europe would be presented with a fait accompli. Even then, of course, localization of the conflict was by no means guaranteed.[18]

Instead, the Austrian leadership chose to frame a long and careful ultimatum to Serbia. Preparation was held up by technical problems until mid-July. But by that time the French president was scheduled to be in Petersburg, allowing close coordination between France and Russia in responding to the crisis. Publication of the ultimatum was therefore further postponed so that Petersburg would not learn of it until after Poincaré had set sail for France. When the Austrian ultimatum finally appeared at 6 P.M. on July 23, Europe had for the most part forgotten about the Austrian Archduke, and by the time of the conciliatory Serbian reply on July 25, it was becoming clear, at least to the foreign offices of the major powers, both that the Austrian action was premeditated and that Berlin must have had a hand in it.

At this point, Bethmann Hollweg's strategy of limiting the conflict began to look implausible, and attention in Berlin shifted, not toward finding a way out of the crisis, but rather to delaying German military preparations long enough so that Russia could be made to look the aggressor. This was the crux of German policy in the final days of the crisis—to delay German war preparations until Russia had announced a general mobilization, and then to blame Russia for starting the war that Germany now sought. The purpose was both to persuade Britain to remain neutral, since it was understood that British policy would never back Russian aggression, and, more crucially, to unify the German people. When Germany entered the war, there is no doubt that the populace believed it was being called upon to defend Germany's existence against the Slavic onslaught.

For the Entente nations, the first clear sign that a major crisis was upon them was the Austrian ultimatum to Serbia on July 23. The forty-eight-hour time limit attached to it was not designed to give them a great deal of room for maneuver. Already by late July 25 Eyre Crowe in the British Foreign Office had discerned the crux of the situation: "The point that matters is whether Germany is or is not absolutely determined to have this war now." Yet he added: "There is still the chance that she can be made to hesitate, if she can be induced to apprehend that the war will find England by the side of France and Russia." The "one effective way of bringing this hope to the German government without absolutely committing us definitely at this stage," Crowe advised, was to mobilize the fleet at the first sign that other powers were mobilizing and to inform the French and Russian governments that Britain had decided upon this course. This, said Crowe, "may conceivably make

Germany realize the seriousness of the danger to which she would be exposed if England took part in the war." Instead, however, Grey temporized, asking Germany to persuade Austria to extend the time limit. The Germans made a show of receptiveness to this suggestion, but in fact Grey's proposal was deliberately held up in Berlin until after the ultimatum had expired. Russian requests for an extension were similarly deflected. All the while Jagow, the German secretary of state, repeatedly affirmed (utterly falsely) that Germany had no foreknowledge of the Austrian action.

Russia had from the first resolved to take a firm stand in the crisis, "even," as Tsar Nicholas stated, "if it should prove necessary to proclaim a mobilisation and open hostilities." At stake was Russia's whole policy in the Near East—her prestige in the Balkan states and by virtue of that her access to the Straits, through which most of her grain was exported. Though Russia opted for a firm stance, two points must be stressed. First, while supporting Serbia, Russia urged a conciliatory response, advising Serbia in the event of an Austrian invasion not to resist but rather to submit the question to other powers for arbitration. According to the Russian charge d'affaires in Belgrade, moreover, the Serbians in replying to Austria's ultimatum would "meet all demands if they are in the slightest degree compatible with the dignity of an independent state." Grey, when he saw the Serbian reply, called it "the greatest humiliation an independent state has ever been subjected to" and expressed his disappointment to Vienna that Austria "treated the Serbian reply as if it had been a decided refusal to comply with [her] wishes."

Second, even though Russian officials calculated that a firm response might lead to war with Germany, they continued to seek a peaceful solution to the crisis to the very end. The firm line was taken in no small measure because previous experience with Germany—particularly in the annexation crisis of 1909—had persuaded the Russian government that even wholesale appeasement would not necessarily prevent war. Since the turn of the century, all three Entente powers had learned from experience that graceful concessions by no means guaranteed a relenting in Berlin's demands. For example, when the French Prime Minister

Rouvier acceded to a German ultimatum demanding the resignation of Delcasse, the French foreign minister, during the first Moroccan crisis in 1905, the Germans, far from agreeing to a settlement, insisted upon an international conference to negotiate further concessions from France. Russia had suffered similarly brusque treatment by Berlin when she sought mediation from Germany over Austria's annexation of Bosnia and Hercegovina in 1909. The British foreign secretary had learned parallel lessons in the arms negotiations with Germany. It was from such experiences with Germany that the Triple Entente had gradually taken shape. Germany's sense of "encirclement" was largely the product of such aggressiveness on her own part in diplomatic dealings with other powers. "Germany," Berghahn notes, "had 'circled herself out' of the great power concert."

On July 26 the Russian Foreign Minister Sazanov attempted to develop an informal mediation proposal with Berlin's ambassador in Petersburg, which was rejected by Germany and Austria. Russian requests for mediation, including a request that the question be put before the Court of Arbitration at the Hague, continued to the end, and Russia even attempted to open a new round of talks with Vienna on July 31, after the Russian general mobilization was already in progress.

French policy, meanwhile, was hobbled by the fact that the French leadership was, in John Keiger's phrase, "literally and metaphorically at sea" during most of the crisis. This, of course, was a consequence of the Central Powers' planning. Poincaré and his entourage departed from Russia on the *France* on July 23 before hearing of the Austrian ultimatum, and arrived at Dunkirk on July 29. Paleologue, Paris's ambassador in Petersburg, gave firm assurances to Sazanov of French backing in the crisis, and much was made for a long time of Paleologue's encouragements. Nonetheless, historians now tend to agree that he was merely reiterating the mutually understood terms of the Entente between Russia and France, and at all events Sazanov showed no signs of wishing for war.

For a long time it was claimed that the news of Russian general mobilization, received in Berlin around noon on July 31, provoked German mobilization and, since German plans drew no distinction between mobilization and attack, triggered world war. Thus, it was argued, delay in the Russian general mobilization might conceivably have diffused the crisis. This argument has recently been revived, with some qualifications, by Steven Van Evera.[19]

Yet the weight of evidence goes utterly against this supposition. The argument was originally made on the invalid assumption that the Russian general mobilization constituted a genuine threat, or at least a provocation, to Germany. On July 28, Austria-Hungary declared war on Serbia, and shelling of Belgrade was begun. Only at this point did Russia order a mobilization—and then a partial one, directed against Austria rather than both Austria and Germany. Notification of the Russian partial mobilization reached Berlin on July 29. On August 1, following the subsequent Russian order for general mobilization and German declaration of war on Russia, a press spokesman for the German Foreign Ministry declared: "Russia alone forces a war on Europe which nobody has wanted except Russia; the full force of responsibility falls on Russia alone."

Yet Berlin's military representative in Petersburg had indicated quite clearly on July 30 that Russian preparations were defensive: "I have the impression that they have mobilised because without having aggressive intentions they are afraid of what will happen and that they are now frightened of what they have done." That the German chancellor himself understood the significance, political and military, of the Russian preparations is clear from his remarks at the Prussian ministry of state on the same day. "Although Russia had proclaimed a mobilisation," Bethmann Hollweg explained, "its mobilisation measures could not be compared with those of the west European [powers].... Russia did not want war, it had been forced by Austria to take this step." When Bethmann Hollweg fought with the generals to delay the German general mobilization until after the Russian general mobilization was ordered, his aim was simply to make Russia *appear* the aggressor. On July 27, the chancellor had insisted to the Kaiser: "In all events Russia must ruthlessly be put into the wrong." Reflecting agreement with this formula, Moltke telegraphed the Austrian chief of staff on July 30: "Wait for Russian mobilisation; Austria must be preserved, must mobilise immediately against Russia, Germany will mobilise. Italy must be compelled by compensations to fulfil its alliance obligations."

Preliminary military preparations were already underway in Germany, but Bethmann succeeded in persuading the generals to delay the order for German general mobilization until noon on July 31. When news of the Russian mobilization order came—as it turns out, only five minutes before the generals' deadline, at 11:55 a.m. on the 31st—the German reaction was not fear but relief. The following day, as the Foreign Ministry sought publicly to shift blame to Russia, there was rejoicing in government circles in Berlin. Moltke later recalled of August 1: "There was, as I said, an atmosphere of happiness." Admiral von Muller recorded in his diary on the same day: "The mood is brilliant. The government has managed to make us appear the attacked."

Would removal of the pretext provided by the Russian general mobilization have averted war? Van Evera implies as much when he says:

> ...British leaders were unaware that German mobilization meant war, hence that peace required Britain to restrain Russia from mobilizing first.... This British ignorance reflected German failure to explain clearly to the Entente that mobilization did indeed mean war—German leaders had many opportunities during the July crisis to make this plain, but did not do so. We can only guess why Germany was silent....

Of those who have examined the records of this period, Van Evera is perhaps alone in having to "guess" why the Reich passed up so many "opportunities" to inform the Entente powers of its military secrets during the July crisis. To say merely that mobilization "meant" war for Germany is to obscure the violation of diplomatic convention implicit in the German plan of responding to Russian mobilization with an immediate attack, through neutral Belgium, on France. "Let it never be admitted," Churchill wrote in 1929 of German planning, "that mobilisation involves war or justifies the other side in declaring war. Mobilisation justifies only counter-mobilisation and further parley."[20] Such, moreover, was the understanding among statesmen in 1914.

To hold Britain somehow accountable for failing to advise Russia not to mobilize, by suggesting that peace "required" such an action, is to apply a peculiar standard of conduct to international politics. In effect, it is to blame Britain for lacking knowledge that Germany deliberately withheld from her. By the conventions of diplomacy there was no reason to believe that Germany would respond to Russian mobilization with an immediate attack. In his dispatch to Buchanan in Petersburg on July 25, Grey assumed, not unnaturally, that the crisis would likely get as far as mobilization of Austria and Russia against one another before a solution could be found. The idea was that mediation might then be introduced to solve the dispute.[21]

Grey's error lay in precisely the opposite direction from that implied by Van Evera's theory of a "cult of the offensive." It was not that Britain was insufficiently accommodating to Germany; it was that she was too accommodating. The whole British posture toward Russia was to counsel delay and restraint, predicated on the belief that Austria, under German persuasion, might relent. But by the time the Tsar ordered general mobilization, German military preparations were already underway, and Serbia was actually under attack. Britain was in no position to advise Russia's leaders against their better judgment not to take steps which they deemed essential to their country's safety. The power of the German armies and the relative rapidity with which they could be deployed were well known; the Russian mobilization was notoriously sluggish by contrast. In return for a delay, it is likely that Russia would have demanded a signal of unambiguous support from Britain— precisely the kind of support that Grey, cleaving to his preferred role as mediator between the coalitions, did not feel in a position to give. Why take such risks, at any rate, especially when no one outside the German government had reason to suspect that mobilization as such would lead immediately to war?

Germany kept her plans secret from other powers—but for a definite and obvious purpose. Only if one assumes (as Van Evera seems to) that Germany was willing to avert war or wished to cooperate with the Entente powers to diffuse the crisis—and nothing suggests that German leaders had any such intentions—does it make sense to propose that she should have revealed the information. (Even then, who can imagine the German Reich unfolding the details of the Schlieffen plan—which the Reich would not even share with its Austro-Hungarian ally—for all to see? The whole concept verges on the absurd.) Rather than reveal the Schlieffen plan, Germany might as easily have refrained from executing it. Only a kind of stubborn insistence that the key to the crisis lay in mistaken "perceptions" would lead one to place such stress on exchanges of information alone. At the same time, to blame the secrecy of the Schlieffen plan on the international system or a generalized "cult of the offensive" in which all powers shared is to overlook the obvious fact that only one power—in collaboration with its allies—secretly dispensed with the distinction between war and mobilization and secretly maneuvered toward war while other powers sought peace. Like so much commentary in this vein on Sarajevo, Van Evera's formulation of the problem simply fails to comprehend the political dimension of the conflict and the seriousness of the German intent.

Such problems aside, however, there is an even more straightforward indication that delay of the Russian general mobilization would have been unavailing: even before news of it reached Berlin on July 31, Bethmann Hollweg had drawn up yet another ultimatum demanding cessation of all military preparations on Russia's part. The aim quite obviously was to use the inevitable Russian refusal as a pretext to go to war. Van Evera himself is forced to concede that the effect of the Russian order has been exaggerated: "Germany apparently decided to attack on learning of Russian partial mobilization, before Russian full mobilization was known in Germany. This suggests that the role of 'inflexible' Russian plans in causing the war is overblown...." Even here Van Evera clings tenaciously to his "action-reaction" paradigm. The German government had, we must remember, envisioned the likelihood of war from the beginning of the crisis. Preliminary plans for German mobilization had been completed as early as July 18, and on July 27, two days before the Russian partial mobilization, Berlin was poised and waiting. As Admiral von Müller noted on that day: "Tendency of our policy: keep quiet, letting Russia put herself in the wrong, but then not shying away from war." In short, that by July 30 Germany would have gone to war in any event seems virtually assured; most recent analyses have coalesced around this view.

Deterrence "Fails"?

The impulse to find a solution to the crisis in a delay of the Russian general mobilization owes more to the conviction that peace lies down the road of accommodation than to any detailed appreciation of the July crisis. But the question remains: Were there actions within the reach of the Entente powers that might have prevented the outbreak of World War I?

The tendency has been to assume the answer to these questions of necessity lies outside the traditional framework of deterrence. Indeed, the lesson usually drawn from Sarajevo is that in 1914 not only deterrence, but the very logic of deterrence "failed." "There is no mystery about the outbreak of the First World War," A.J.P. Taylor once asserted, a bit perversely. "The deterrent failed to deter. This was to be expected sooner or later. A deterrent may work ninety-nine times out of a hundred. On the hundredth occasion it produces a catastrophe."[22] Yet this is precisely the "mystery" that keeps Sarajevo alive in our minds: the inexplicable failure of deterrence—an especially troubling lesson, if proven accurate, for the nuclear era. The mysteriousness, however, depends on assumptions about the crisis and German intentions discredited by recent historical investigation. In fact, the framework of deterrence is capable of explaining fairly adequately why the July crisis led to war and of pointing toward actions that might have been taken to avert the catastrophe.

German policy in the Sarajevo crisis was a response not so much to the strength as to the weakness of the Triple Entente. In the wake of the war, there was a tendency among British and American commentators to blame the conflict on the tightness of the opposing coalitions. This was less a conclusion drawn from observation than a restatement of the longstanding liberal conviction that alliances are by nature bellicose arrangements, likely to result in war, a belief that one can trace back through nineteenth-century liberalism to the French enlightenment. The same assumption resurfaces in Van Evera's analysis, which speaks of "the general tendency of alliances toward tightness and offensiveness in an offense-dominated world." But this is simply a misconception. Not only did the Entente, as we have seen, explicitly eschew an "offensive" posture, but also, as Taylor himself has pointed out, "the existing alliances were all precarious." Britain's commitment to France, let alone to Russia, was far from open or obviously assured. A more unambiguous British commitment to France in itself would have done much to undermine German confidence in success. As German planning suggests, the very weakness of the Entente created incentives for a high-risk game, since the possibility that Britain would fail to support her putative friends made the prospects of both diplomatic and military victories all the more plausible. The Triple Entente was no NATO. The weakness and elusiveness of its arrangements was especially clear to Russia's Foreign Minister Sazanov, who lamented to his ambassador in London in February 1914 that:

> [W]orld peace will only be assured the day the Triple Entente, whose existence can no more be proved than the existence of the sea monster, is transformed into a defensive alliance without secret clauses and when this fact is publicly announced in all the newspapers of the world. On that day the danger of German hegemony will finally disappear.

Buchanan, the British ambassador in Petersburg, endorsed the logic of Sazanov's analysis.

Moreover, we know the hope of British neutrality in a Continental war figured importantly in German calculations. Fear that Britain might fight alongside France was a major factor holding Germany's leaders back in the spring of 1914, even as the generals were urging war. "Our people," Moltke complained to Conrad in May, referring to his civilian colleagues in the government, "unfortunately still expect a declaration from Britain that it will not join in. This declaration Britain will never make." The only point in the July crisis at which Bethmann actually sought, albeit half-heartedly, to reverse the headlong plunge to war came in the early hours of July 30, after he learned from his ambassador in London that Britain would almost certainly not remain neutral. The chancellor telegraphed Tschirschky, Berlin's ambassador in Vienna, urging that he press "most urgently and impressively" for the "acceptance of mediation" by Vienna. In a second message sent a few minutes later, he warned that Germany, while "ready to fulfil the obligations of our alliance...must decline to be drawn wantonly into a world conflagration by Vienna." But the shelling of Belgrade was already underway, and the Austrians, having up to this point been continually pressed and prodded by Germany to go forward, were unwilling now to stop. The news of London's attitude had come too late. Bethmann's reaction to it suggests that an earlier and firmer signal might well have had effect. The example of the Agadir crisis of 1911, when the clear and early war threat embodied in Lloyd George's bellicose Mansion House speech shocked German authorities and threw cold water on German planning for war, supports that view.

Finally, there is the attitude of William himself, who, on the basis of a selective interpretation of a remark of the English king, had chosen to believe throughout the July crisis that British neutrality was assured. It is significant—and also rather typical— that when the Kaiser learned that Britain was in fact to be drawn into the war, he felt that he had been deceived. But far from engaging in fraud, Britain had merely been characteristically indecisive. The point is that her diplomacy failed to translate her military assets into a "political power factor" at a crucial time.

A more open British commitment to the Entente, and especially to France—in effect, the conversion of the Entente into an open defensive alliance—would have enforced a limit on German ambitions; in the absence of such a standing commitment, an early signal of British resolve, such as was advised by Crowe, might have had the same effect. However, the dominant liberal assumptions about foreign affairs prevented Britain from exercising either option. A firm alliance with Russia was politically impossible both because Russia was regarded as an illiberal regime, and because alliances themselves were regarded by British liberals as inherently provocative. For the Anglo-American liberal of 1914, there was as yet no such thing as a purely defensive, or NATO-style alliance. It would require not one but two world wars for liberal thought to absorb the truth that a straightforward alliance or coalition of states committed to maintaining the status quo could be a major force for preserving peace. (To judge from Van Evera's argument, the lesson may still be uncertainly learnt.)

During the crisis itself, the idea that a firm and early commitment to the Entente might have forestalled German aggression was not lost on all members of the British government. Yet an attempt to provide such a commitment would have split the cabinet irreparably and brought the government down in the midst of the international crisis. Even had it been possible, the effectiveness of such a commitment would have depended upon the credibility as well as the earliness of the signal. Had the Germans been convinced of British resolve by May, it would have proved perhaps more of a deterrent than the gestures that Crowe advised once the crisis was actually underway. Whether the latter action would have deterred the war is still disputed by historians.[23]

In any case, to lay the groundwork for more decisive action at Sarajevo, Grey would have had to embark much earlier on a long process of public education, instilling in the British populace a clear understanding of the political issues at stake. The British public would need to have been made to see the Entente in a light somewhat similar to that in which Americans now see NATO. Such notions would have gone against radical sentiment in Grey's own party. There was, at any rate, a strong disinclination to engage in such public education, traceable both to anxiety over preserving Liberal party unity and to the distaste of Foreign Office officials for the task of accounting for policy to an uninformed and emotional public. Sarajevo was among the first tests of the ability of modern democracies to conduct foreign policy in a crisis pregnant with the possibility of war, and the failure of Britain to respond effectively was in no small part due to a failure to adapt foreign policy to the exigencies of democratic rule, to shape a public mandate for policies essential to Britain's long-range survival and prosperity. This problem is one that the present-day democracies have by no means entirely solved.

To all these circumstances must be added the purely military consideration that, as has usually been true throughout history, everybody, and especially the aggressors, expected a short war—a decisive conflict of several weeks or, at most, months in duration. The "short-war illusion" was decisive in German military planning. The Germans were by no means alone in failing to understand that the military advantage in modern warfare had shifted decisively from the offensive to the defensive, and that consequently a long war of attrition was almost inevitable. But Germany alone sought to exploit the presumed offensive advantage. Whatever their costs on the battlefield, French offensive battle tactics in themselves posed no threat to the peace; German offensive foreign policy did.

Nations do not launch wars because they are afraid, but because they are confident that they will gain more by resorting to force than by refraining from doing so. This was true no less in 1914 than in other cases. It is a fact that Germany was fearful in a sense; fearful not of any immediate attack, but of losing her current advantageous position—"afraid," as Grey later put it, "that she would be afraid." It was by no means clear that in three years' time Germany would be the victor in a Continental war. The generals envisioned a future conflict with Russia as a certainty, and Russia's power was growing. But, as Fischer notes, in Bethmann Hollweg's discussion of the problem, there is no expectation of Russian aggression, merely a suggestion that if a war occurred three years hence Germany would be at a disadvantage.

At all events, to understand the effects of the German fear one must understand how it interacted with the German confidence of victory, which was, after all, the indispensable ingredient of a war-making policy. If Germany were simply fearful, if it were clear that in the "roll of the iron dice" the odds were against her, then even with her predisposition to aggression she doubtless would have refrained from precipitating a war, as she had in 1911. Doubtless, had Germany's leadership been able to foresee the actual outcome of the war, they would have been far less eager to bring it on. But her leaders, and her generals in particular, were confident. What deterrence proposes to offer the potential aggressor is a picture, in effect a discouraging "snapshot" of the future if a power chooses war. The snapshot viewed by the German leadership was manifestly incorrect.

Indeed, World War I revealed a pattern that would pave the road to fighting more than once in the twentieth century: the systematic tendency of democracies to appear weaker and less resolute than they really are in periods leading up to war. This pattern was evident in World War II, in Korea, and, more recently, in the 1982 Argentine invasion of the Falkland Islands. Anti-militarist forces in the democracies tend to constrain policy in ways that suggest to more militaristic and authoritarian powers that the democracies lack the wherewithal to resist. Ironically, once democracies perceive themselves under attack, they encounter little trouble in mobilizing public opinion, and nationalism takes on a life of its own. Once galvanized for war, they have generally proved to be formidable enemies. This pattern tends to make war more rather than less likely, since it encourages aggression on the part of ambitious non-democratic states. Such is the paradox: In the twentieth century, those powers least prone to choose war as a vehicle of policy have also been *a fortiori* the least prone to take the steps necessary to prevent other powers from choosing it.

As for the notion that "arms races cause wars," the least that can be said is that it gives a completely distorted picture of the events that culminated in war in 1914. It obscures the source both of the arms race and of the war itself, which lay in German ambitions and conscious decisions made by the German Reich. Eyre Crowe was correct about the Sarajevo crisis almost from the start: the key question was always whether Germany wanted war and was willing to risk it, and whether Entente powers, Britain in particular, could take actions that would render such risks unacceptable. The First World War did not result from any "accident"; war came in 1914 for the relatively simple reason that a hegemonic state sought to expand its influence in the world and was persuaded by the apparent momentary weakness and indecision of its opponents to do so by violent means. (In this respect, Sarajevo differs sharply from the Cuban missile crisis, where, according to at least one report, the Soviet leadership, acutely aware of its inferior capabilities, had no thought of war and sought from the beginning an avenue of retreat.[24])

Ten years after World War I, Churchill noted concerning the thorny issue of war responsibility:

> Disputes as to responsibility for bringing about conditions which led to various wars are endless. But mankind will be wise in the future to take as the paramount criterion of war guilt the sending of the main armies by any State across its frontier line, and to declare that whoever does this puts himself irretrievably in the wrong.

The accurate, and also common-sense, statement of the situation was that Germany had caused the war. For this basic fact, the arms race paradigm substituted the abstraction that "nationalism caused the war" or "militarism caused the war" or "the arms race caused the war" or, to use the latest formulation, "the 'cult of the offensive' caused the war." But neither "nationalism" nor "militarism" nor "the cult of the offensive" nor the impulse to improve her fortunes by amassing arms existed in other regimes as in Germany; nor, given the constitution of the democracies, is it likely that such forces could have taken control.

The error of the arms race paradigm lay in generalizing from the German case to the other powers; this derived in turn from a tendency to abstract "militarism" artificially from the particular political setting in which it took hold and became overmastering. The paradigm treated "militarism," inaccurately, as a force to which all powers were, if not equally subject, then equally susceptible in peacetime—in short, as a kind of communicable disease. Behind this one can sense an almost scientific impulse to identify, isolate, and banish (or at least control) a factor alleged to be at the root of political conflict between states. It amounts to little less than a denial of politics itself, a simple refusal to accept that the phenomenon of the hegemonic or aggressive state is an elemental reality of political life, to be understood on its own terms, irreducible to other factors.

But the arms race thesis went hand in hand from the outset with the idea of rejecting or transcending politics. Those who spoke of preventing war by ending arms races in the 1920s and 1930s also spoke of the dawn of a new international order in which, as Grey put it, "war must be ruled out." The two ideas were closely linked. Those who hesitated to blame Germany emphasized instead that the war was "the child of the European anarchy, of the outworn system of sovereign states."[25] Consonant with the liberal vision of politics, rather than blame the problem on an aggressive or wanton state, the arms race paradigm blamed it on states and governments in general, on states and governments as such—on the very mechanism, the very nature of politics.

Ironically, at the moment when war broke out in 1914, it was widely read as a devastating indictment of liberal assumptions about international affairs. In a remarkable gesture on August 8, 1914, *The Nation*, Britain's leading radical journal, printed what amounted to a repudiation of the liberal-pacifist foreign policy vision:

> Who in the future will pay attention to the *Daily News*...the *Manchester Guardian* and other journals of the same stamp? These idealists...who refuse to look reality in the face and prefer to be deceived and to deceive their followers.... Who will heed when the Lord Courtneys and Wedgwoods and the Trevelyans presume to air their baby views on so complicated a subject as foreign politics and our duties toward our friends and allies? I venture to say, after what has happened, no one.

And yet by 1919, the same war that once was regarded as an indictment of the liberal vision of foreign policy was treated as the most compelling argument for its implementation. In the end, the notion that war had been caused by the arms race was less an observation based on events than a complicated reaffirmation of the once-discredited liberal-pacifist vision of international politics.

Yet in setting the framework for efforts to prevent another war, the arms race paradigm pointed the democracies in exactly the wrong direction. It taught that democratic Britain had been too militaristic before the war, when the truth was that she had been not quite firm or vigilant enough. It encouraged at best a certain insouciance about military power, implying that deterrence was an inherently dangerous or simply unnecessary arrangement, something to be transcended or dispensed with—when the real lesson of Sarajevo was that hegemonic states could be prevented from unleashing war only by ensuring that deterrence and defensive alliances remained unambiguously strong. From the standpoint of British liberalism, such a conclusion would have amounted to an unpalatable acknowledgement that power politics was—and is—a permanent feature of the human condition.

Notes

[1]Edward Grey, *Twenty-five Years 1892–1916* (Hodder and Stoughton, 1925).

[2]See Ole R. Holsti and Robert C. North, "The History of Human Conflict," in Elton B. McNeil, ed., *The Nature of Human Conflict* (Prentice-Hall, 1965); and Dean G. Pruitt and Richard C. Snyder, eds., *Theory and Research on the Causes of War* (Prentice-Hall, 1969). Snyder and Van Evera's research has been summarized in *International Security* (Summer 1984), reprinted in book form as Steven E. Miller, ed., *Military Strength and the Origins of the First World War* (Princeton University Press, 1985).

[3]Fritz Fischer, *Germany's Aims in the First World War* (W.W. Norton, 1967); *War of Illusions* (Chatto & Windus, 1975); and *World Power or Decline: The Controversy over Germany's Aims in the First World War* (W.W. Norton, 1974). For good accounts of the events of the period, see also V.R. Berghahn, *Germany and the Approach of War in 1914* (St. Martin's Press, 1973); E.L. Woodward, *Great Britain and the German Navy* (London, 1935); and Imanuel Geiss, ed., *July 1914 the Outbreak of the First World War: Selected Documents* (B.T. Batsford, 1967).

[4]See Geoffrey Blainey, *The Causes of Wars* (The Free Press, 1973), and Donald Kagan, "World War I, World War II, World War III," *Commentary* (March 1987).

[5]See Quincy Wright, *A Study of War*, 2nd ed. (University of Chicago Press, 1965).

[6]Coit D. Blacker and Gloria Duffy, eds., *International Arms Control: Issues and Agreements*, 2nd ed. (Stanford University Press, 1984).

[7]A good guide to pre-war radical thinking is A.J. Morris, *Radicalism Against War, 1906–1914: The Advocacy of Peace and Retrenchment* (Longmans, 1972).

[8]For specifics of German and British naval plans, see Jonathan Steinberg, *Yesterday's Deterrent: Tirpitz and the Birth of the German Battle Fleet* (Mac-Donald, 1965) and Arthur J. Marder, *From the Dreadnought to Scapa Flow: the Royal Navy in the Fisher Era, 1904–1919*. Vol. 1 *The Road to War 1904–1919* (Oxford University Press, 1961), as well as Berghahn *op. cit.*

[9]Jonathan Steinberg, "The Copenhagen Complex" *Journal of Contemporary History* (July 1966).

[10]Winston S. Churchill, *The World Crisis* (Charles Scribner's Sons, 1931).

[11]For the situation in France, see Jean-Jacques Becker, *1914: Comment les Français sont entrés dans la guerre* (Presses de la Foundation Nationale des Sciences Politiques, 1977); Raoul Giradet, ed., *Le nationalisme français 1871–1914* (Armand Colin, 1966); and John F.V. Keiger, *France and the Origins of the First World War* (St. Martin's Press, 1983). For the situation in Russia, see D.C.B. Lieven, *Russia and the Origins of the First World War* (St. Martin's Press, 1983).

[12]George F. Kennan, "World War I; Then II; Then..." *New York Times*, November 11, 1984. Kennan's recent scholarly volumes on the origins of World War I are imbued with the revisionist outlook. See Paul Seabury and Patrick Glynn, "Kennan: The Historian as Fatalist," *The National Interest* (Winter 1985/86).

[13]In Dwight E. Lee, ed. *The Outbreak of the First World War: Causes and Responsibilities*, 4th ed. (D.C. Heath and Co., 1975).

[14]See Clive Trebilcock, "Legends of the British Armaments Industry 1890–1914," *Journal of Contemporary History* (October 1970).

[15]See Michael R. Gordon, "Domestic Conflict and the Origins of the First World War: The British and the German Cases," *Journal of Modern History* 46 (1974).

[16]In collaboration with Eugenia V. Nomikos, North has advanced a slight-ly revised version of the original Holsti-North thesis which takes Fischer's work to some degree into account. While acknowledging that success in diffusing crises requires all parties to eschew war, they still place their stress on the need to "generate trust" and make pacific intentions clear. See Eugenia V. Nomikos and Robert C. North, *International Crisis: The Outbreak of World War I* (McGill-Queen's University Press, 1976).

[17]Imanuel Geiss, "The Outbreak of the First World War and German War Aims," *Journal of Contemporary History* (July 1966).

[18]This account follows Berghahn over Fischer in taking Bethmann Hollweg's hopes of localizing the conflict more seriously. See also "The Illusion of Limited War" in Konrad H. Jarausch, *The Enigmatic Chancellor:*

Bethmann Hollweg and the Hubris of Imperial Germany (Yale University Press, 1973).

[19]Steven Van Evera, "The Cult of the Offensive and the Origins of the First World War," in Miller, *op. cit.*

[20]Winston S. Churchill, *The Aftermath* (Charles Scribner's Sons, 1929).

[21]See Luigi Albertini, *The Origins of the War of 1914*, 3 Volumes (English trans. Oxford University Press, 1952–57).

[22]A.J.P. Taylor, *War by Time-Table: How the First World War Began* (Mac-Donald, 1969).

[23]See, for example, Zara S. Steiner, *Britain and the Origins of the First World War* (St. Martin's Press, 1977).

[24]Arkady N. Shevchenko, *Breaking with Moscow* (Alfred A. Knopf, 1985).

[25]G.P. Gooch, *Recent Revelations of European Diplomacy* 4th ed. (Longmans, 1940).

PATRICK GLYNN*

Reassessing the Lessons of Sarajevo

Let me begin by sketching what I see as the basic logic of the issue at hand from the standpoint of peace research. It seems to me that for all of us, the logical starting point in approaching these issues is our profound desire to prevent the occurrence of a third world war, which in our time is almost certain to be a nuclear war. I think we all share a recognition that a nuclear war would be an incredible, unparalleled catastrophe.

The question, then, is this: How do we prevent a major war with the Soviet Union? What are the policies most likely to prevent war, to preserve peace with freedom over the long term? What, on the other hand, are the policies most likely to bring on war? To answer that question systematically, we need to know something about how wars are caused and how they are prevented. It is precisely this concern that has inspired Western preoccupation with the causes of war since 1919.

Fundamentally, the question of how wars are caused is a question about human nature and about politics—about how human beings act within politics, what motivates them, what they desire, and what they fear.

Obviously, as the scope of the Research and Studies Program of the United States Institute of Peace suggests, there are many ways to learn about human nature and politics. One can observe human nature, for example, through the lens of modern psychology. One can even construct experiments, as psychologists do from time to time. But in learning about human beings within politics, we are forced to rely heavily on history, on analogies and insights drawn from historical experience. Almost nothing else gives us the range of political experience in its fullness and complexity. However, it would be impossible to devise an experiment that would duplicate the complex array of conditions leading up to a major international crisis or a major war.

We all understand, of course, that historical analogies are rarely perfect. History almost never repeats itself in a literal sense. Still, there are patterns in the way human beings and political regimes behave, and these patterns are derived from certain inherent limits and traits in human nature. Without such patterns and limits, human experience would be an absurdity—"a tale told by an idiot," as Macbeth says, "full of sound and fury, Signifying nothing." In short, there is a recognized coherence to political experience, and the great task of students of politics—and of students of peace—is to understand the basis of this coherence as precisely as we can. Having grasped the underlying nature of politics, we can better predict the outcome of a particular policy or set of policies, and, in this way, we will be in a better position to avoid disasters. That, I think, is the basis of our interest in historical experience from the standpoint of peace research.

In fact, since 1945 our whole approach to deterring war and keeping peace has been guided in large part by historical analogies, and in particular by two powerful ones: the analogy of Munich and the analogy of Sarajevo.

The problem has been that these two analogies have seemed to teach diametrically opposed lessons about the causes of war and the nature of politics. On the one hand, Munich (and by Munich I mean the chain of events roughly from Hitler's accession to power in 1933 to Britain's declaration of war in 1939) taught that disarmament treaties and a diplomacy of conciliation were likely only to aggravate international tensions and invite aggression. Sarajevo, on the other hand, seemed to teach the opposite: the very effort to preserve deterrence by matching or exceeding an ambitious opponent's military capabilities was likely to create a climate conducive to war, which then, amid an international crisis, might occur inadvertently or accidentally.

All of this lent what might be called an element of mysticism to Western diplomacy. Given the contradiction between Sarajevo and Munich, there was no logical solution to the problem of preserving peace. Diplomacy became a matter of balancing occult forces—reconciling, as it were, the yin and yang of Sarajevo and Munich. Responsible statesmen like Henry Kissinger knew from common sense and realism that they had to preserve a favorable balance of power vis-à-vis the Soviet Union, but they also knew, or thought they knew, on the basis of the Sarajevo experience, that the very effort to preserve a favorable balance was risky and dangerous and might itself lead to war—since arms races create tensions and foster conditions conducive to crisis and war. Obviously this risk, if it were real, had to be taken seriously in the presence of nuclear weapons. So in addition to playing the power game as realistically as possible, Kissinger and others also made a huge, and somewhat contradictory, investment in arms control. The Kissinger example is only one way in which preoccupation with the Sarajevo problem has shaped American policy. Altogether Sarajevo has had a major impact, lending a fundamental ambivalence and uncertainty to Western policy regarding the challenge posed by the Soviet Union.

What I have done in my "Sarajevo Fallacy" article is simply to bring into focus what historians of the First World War have known, remarkably enough, since the early to mid-1960s; namely, that the conventional understanding of the Sarajevo crisis is wrong—that World War I was not in any sense caused by an arms race, that it was not inadvertent or accidental, that Britain and the Entente powers erred, not by responding to the German military challenge in kind, but rather by failing to respond resolutely enough at key moments and by failing to sustain a firm and unified posture over time.

What are the implications of this finding for research into peace? Let me address briefly each of the four issues we have been asked to touch on: the causes of wars, deterrence, arms control, and the special problems of democracies in keeping the peace.

The Causes of Wars   The analysis here suggests that there may be a great deal more unity to the theory of war and peace than we had previously thought. Sarajevo is not, as has been believed, a great anomaly. The lesson of Sarajevo is not fundamentally at odds with the lesson of Munich; on close examination, the lesson of Sarajevo collapses into the lesson of Munich. The two episodes teach basically the same lesson about war and peace. Indeed, there turns out to be a remarkable consistency in the circumstances leading to some of the major wars of this century: World War I, World War II, Korea, and even the Falklands War. In each case, the irresolute and uncertain policies of democracies, fostered in large part by idealistic and antimilitaristic tendencies in those societies, invited aggression from a more militaristic power. In this sense, my article points toward a new and potentially more unified and consistent theory of the causes of wars, at least of the type of war that concerns us most.

Deterrence   I believe that a reexamination of Sarajevo should relieve a good deal of anxiety prevalent today about deterrence as a tool for keeping the peace. What a reexamination suggests, very simply, is that deterrence does not cause wars. Nations don't cause wars inadvertently by accumulating the military strength to deter them, nations cause wars by failing to match or exceed a rising power's capabilities and resolve. That realization is very important for the West.

Contrary to the rhetoric often heard in the U.S. Congress, new weapons systems on our side do not pose a threat to the peace any more than the British *Dreadnought* was a contributing factor to the causes of World War I. The Soviets will try to overmatch us regardless of what we do. Like the Germans in 1914, they are reacting, not to our deployments, but to their own ambitions.

At any rate, the basic point is that the objective condition of deterrence—not negotiations, not unilateral restraint, not treaties—is the only guarantee of peace in the face of a hegemonic adversary. I should add that political resolve—the apparent willingness to bring one's military forces into play—is as important as the forces themselves.

There is a corollary to deterrence that has to do with the indispensability of alliances. One of the major causes of World War I was the classical liberal-democratic hostility toward alliances, which currently is undergoing an unfortunate revival on both ends of the political spectrum. Geographically and economically, the United States needs NATO and its Asian allies to contain Soviet power, just as Britain needed France and even Russia in 1914. The loss of these alliances, however vexing or inhibiting they may seem to be at times, would be a major disaster for peace.

Arms Control A close examination of the Sarajevo paradigm raises two basic questions about arms control. First, we can see that arms control negotiations were undertaken on a serious scale even before World War I and that they did nothing to slow the growth of German naval and military power. Indeed, as I tried to suggest in my article, they were counterproductive. The failure of the pre-World War I effort when combined with the failure of even more ambitious efforts before World War II does not bode well for our current hopes in this area.

Second, I believe my article raises serious doubts about the validity of the very premises on which the arms control enterprise is based. It is important to recognize that modern arms control theory is intimately tied to the Sarajevo fallacy. The revisionist interpretation of World War I provided the major justification for the disarmament efforts in the 1930s, and, in later years, the justification for arms control theory proper when it emerged in the nuclear age. In the simplest terms, what we are trying to do with arms control is to prevent another Sarajevo, to prevent another world war. When the Reagan administration officially stated that its chief objective in arms control was to "reduce the risk of war," it was calling on the Sarajevo paradigm—the notion that certain force configurations are less stable in a crisis, just as historians once believed that mobilization plans and military timetables were ultimately responsible for the outbreak of war in August 1914. But all of this planning rests on a series of assumptions about Sarajevo and World War I that, as we have seen, are simply incorrect. That is, we are trying to solve a problem that does not exist, and we are doing so in a way that history suggests has tended to weaken, rather than strengthen, the barriers to war. Not only has the classic era of arms control coincided with an enormous growth in Soviet military power, but our commitment to arms control today is clearly undermining our willingness to build and maintain a robust deterrent. Congress continually cites arms control considerations to place unilateral limits on our military capabilities—presumably influenced by the fallacious notion that arming and arms races indirectly cause wars. A basic rethinking of this proposition is clearly in order.

At this point an objection may be raised: What of the special problems posed by nuclear weapons? Do they not present fundamentally different problems from those faced in 1914? Here I would make two points. First, we can't have it both ways. Either historical analogies from the prenuclear period are applicable or they are not. The architects of arms control theory relied heavily on the analogy of 1914 to arrive at their original formulation. It would be inconsistent today to turn around and say that 1914 no longer counts. Indeed, the latest crop of scholars on international security are even more devoted than their predecessors to detailed historical analogies. I am speaking of the work of scholars like Steven Van Evera and Richard C. Snyder on the impact of offensive military doctrines before World War I and so forth. This research is all well and good. The fact is most of us accept the utility of such historical analogies because we understand that while weapons may have changed, human nature and thus politics have not.

The second point I would make is that the belief that nuclear weapons have changed everything is itself a variation on the Sarajevo fallacy—a variation on the notion that weapons have a causal effect on peace and war. The point is that, although weapons may have changed, the fundamental calculus of power remains the same, even in the nuclear age.

The Special Problems of Democracies in Keeping the Peace In a sense, the question of political regimes is as much a methodological point as a substantive issue. One key to penetrating the Sarajevo fallacy is to grasp the critical importance of the distinction among political regimes. It is here that naive views of international politics prove in some ways superior to supposedly more sophisticated ones. Classical liberal-democracy sought to abandon the naive "us versus them," "good guys and bad guys," approach to international affairs—to substitute a more abstract and theoretical outlook, which not only seemed more civilized but also potentially more efficacious. The belief was that by manipulating and controlling forces such as militarism and nationalism (and armaments themselves) one could simply eliminate war as a factor in human affairs. At the root of this supposed sophistication was perhaps an even more fundamental naivete: the notion that the world of nations could be made to operate on the principle of the Golden Rule—for what was the British radical slogan "moderation brings moderation" but a variation on the Golden Rule? This notion went hand in hand with a certain ethnocentricism, a failure to recognize that other cultures and other governments might have fundamentally different outlooks and priorities from one's own.

In abandoning the naive moral formula that blamed Germany for aggression, Western liberal democrats sacrificed a great deal of practical insight into the origins of the war. By the same token, much of the misdiagnosis of the arms race that has governed policy in recent times has its roots in a failure to understand the fundamental differences—in behavior, in outlook, and in ambitions—between a hegemonic and a status quo power, between totalitarian or authoritarian regimes and liberal-democratic states. A revival of the category "regime" is essential, it seems to me, for understanding the real causes and mechanisms of the arms race.

Democracies do have special problems keeping the peace, precisely because they are more peaceable than the states that threaten them.

PART II

Commentators Respond to Glynn

On the Significance of Sarajevo and Arms Control

Let me begin with an apology. I have hardly a single intelligent word to say about the First World War. As a student, I always found medieval theology much less arcane than the revisionist controversies about the First World War. I am more exercised, instead, by the implications of Patrick Glynn's interpretation of that war, by his understanding of the nature of arms control and the magnitude of its role in the reduction of the risk of nuclear war. I shall say briefly what I find valuable about Glynn's analysis, what I think he has indeed established to the benefit of all his readers; then I'll set out two or three areas in which he and I would differ. I should add, by way of alluding to my misgivings about some of Glynn's ideas, that I came away from my medieval studies with a promise never to use the word *theology* pejoratively.

I think Glynn has established three points very nicely. First, he has made life much more difficult for the doctrine of technological reductionism, or more concretely (in the language of today's technology) ballistic reductionism. That is to say, he has established that weapons do not make war, but that people do. I concur with him in his suggestion that the primary characteristic of war, for the purpose of understanding its origins, is what might be called, a little pretentiously, human intentionality. War is the product of political designs and strategic calculations, that is, of politics. War is not simply the inexorable and somnambulistic issue of dumb but deadly arsenals, of whatever the particular state of weaponry happens to be at the time.

Having commented on this first critical matter on which Glynn and I would agree, I must add that I detect at points in his argument a certain overweening confidence in the human control of events. That men can will a conflict does not mean that men can control one. The refutation of technological reductionism must not have the effect of obscuring the significant effect that technology does have on the outbreak of war, the conduct of war, the termination of war. Even if weapons do not start wars, weapons have something to do with how and why people start wars. Accidental wars are still possible, either as a result of political misunderstanding, that is, of human accident, or because of electronic misunderstanding, that is, because of technological accident.

Second, I think that Glynn has established that disarmament does not necessarily lead to disarmament; that what he calls the *action-reaction phenomenon* does not always obtain; that action sometimes leads to action and not to reaction; that action-reaction could also, as a result of misunderstandings of all kinds, appear as reaction-action; and so on. His case study of the First World War seems to show that the disarmers who believe that the logical response to the disarmament of the one side is the disarmament of the other side—that disarmament is not so much a policy as a logic—are not correct. Again, he may be right about that war. His observation is certainly right about what I take to be the thinly veiled subtext of his paper, that is, the competition in strategic forces between the United States and the Soviet Union since the early 1970s. I don't think that anybody in this room needs to hear Harold Brown's apothegm ("We build, the Soviets build. We stop building, the Soviets build") again—or, indeed, that anybody in this room would substantially take issue with it.

Third, and this point certainly needs no belaboring here, I think Glynn has established the political, strategic, philosophical, and moral necessity of armament. I accept his conclusion that perceived weakness in weaponry has a place in the origins of war; that in a world characterized by a balance of power, a weak state may be a temptation a strong state cannot long withstand.

So far, my praise. There are, however, a number of significant issues on which Glynn and I differ. The first is the link he draws between something he calls the *arms race* (I don't mean to saddle him with that cliché) and arms control. Simply put, the proposition that weapons do not cause war says nothing whatsoever about what need there is to control those weapons. Even if arms races don't start wars, we still need arms control in two ways. First, and I'll return to this in a moment, there is at least one sense in which arms control can indeed reduce the risk of war, and that is the variety of arms control that consists in the elimination of certain types or classes of weapons systems from the arsenals of *both* parties. Such arms control has a very practical consequence: it can eliminate certain options or courses of action that would be open to policy makers in a crisis. Whatever the justice of the other side—however much men and not weapons start wars—such arms control will ensure that certain weapons will simply not be available to use.

I presume that we all agree that in the nuclear age this point is not trivial. (I hear a great deal lately about the "post-nuclear age," but I must confess that I don't see it.) Surely we all agree that there are weapons or weapons systems that are more inhibiting and less inhibiting to use; that in a crisis or conflict the absence or unavailability of a relatively inhibiting, but spectacularly lethal (not just to *them*, but also to *us*), weapon to a belligerent nation would contribute significantly to the prevention or the termination of war; and that a particular contribution will have been the result of arms control and nothing else. Or shall we leave it to the good nature and good judgment of a general to stay his hand in the middle of a nuclear conflict? Remember, human intentionality is not the same thing as human rationality.

I concede that the kind of arms control that I have described— and it is, of course, a kind of arms control that has been practiced by the United States and the Soviet Union, if not often enough (its monument is the Anti-Ballistic Missile [ABM] Treaty)—takes place, from the standpoint of the day-to-day maintenance of national security, "at the margin," as policy people like to say. In the nuclear age, however, the margin is not marginal. Civilization may one day be saved by the margin.

So at least in the sense I've discussed, arms control can play a role in reducing or preventing war. But there's another sense in which it can, too. I do not accept the tone or the historical implications of Glynn's comments on arms control. I detect a tendency—perhaps surprising in a historical exercise—toward the creation of a straw man.

In the history of nuclear arms control, there have been two schools or types of approaches to arms control. There has been an eschatological notion of arms control and a managerial notion of arms control. The eschatological notion of arms control (according to which arms control is all that is necessary to prevent nuclear war, and therefore peace is merely a matter of the negotiation of quantitative reductions among weapons systems) is a caricature of what the position of real arms control has been in the nuclear age.

There are some people, of course (many of them in Stockholm), who do seem to hold this eschatological notion of arms control. The position that Glynn calls theology does exist. But is it prominent? Has it played a significant role in the theory or the practice of the actual history of the attempt to control weapons? Of course not. I don't see the eschatological view in any White House, Defense Department, Arms Control Disarmament Agency, or State Department in the nuclear age. I certainly do not see it in Washington in the 1980s. My feeling is that Glynn is attacking an easy target—one that is almost off the playing field.

There is, however, a more real and defensible notion of arms control that is entirely compatible with Glynn's (and my) realism: the managerial notion, which understands that politics not weapons start wars, which recognizes human agency but doesn't trust it completely. The managerial notion (to use Glynn's odd term, *opprobrium*) is in no sense classically liberal, or naive, or some Panglossian child of an Enlightenment view of human nature (according to which people simply want the best but are confused or led by evil design—or indeed by technology—to the worst). Indeed, the man who believes that the human control of war needs no help or hobbling by arms control is the Panglossian.

Now, this is philosophically not a very sexy position. It certainly lacks grandeur. And politically it is even less sexy:

managerialism is not for bumper stickers. But it is a fact of history that the role of the arms controller since the 1960s has been to manage a very limited dimension of war and peace, that dimension being the weaponry available to the protagonists. The arms controller is a calibrator of a balance—no more, no less.

This limited view of arms control is not an insignificant one, and it has prevailed in the real world. I do not see that Glynn's "Sarajevo Fallacy" lays a glove on it. Whatever you think about the merit of particular treaties or specific arms control regimes, it seems to me indisputable that the eschatological notion has not figured prominently in the real world, or greatly influenced it.

Next, I agree that the term *arms race* is an unfortunate one. Obviously the criticism of its usage should be directed mainly to certain precincts of the Left, but I think that Glynn the critic has inadvertently fallen victim to the notion, too. Obviously, again, arms races and weapons do not start wars. But arms races and weapons are generalities. War and peace are a matter of specifics. There are some technologies more conducive to the outbreak of war and some less conducive to the outbreak of war (correcting at all times for the primacy of politics and human decisions and so on). Weapons may not start wars, but some weapons make wars easier to start than others. With respect to the prevention of war, therefore, weapons cannot be considered only quantitatively. And Glynn does so, like some of those he criticizes.

There is also a variety of arms control that has come to be known as qualitative arms control. The classic example of the need for this kind of arms control (it's rather recent to be classic, but I guess that, in a nuclear era, history has been somewhat accelerated) is the Multiple Independently Targetable Reentry Vehicle (MIRV)—more specifically, the failure to control the MIRV. This example perfectly illustrates a technology that, had it been nipped in the bud by a form of qualitative arms control, would not have resulted in an arms race (there has indeed been a MIRV race) or significantly increased the chances for the outbreak of war between the superpowers. MIRV is precisely what you wish a president or a general secretary could not contemplate in a crisis.

It seems perfectly clear to me in the case of MIRV (in the case of Strategic Defense Initiative [SDI], too, though it seems mercifully to have become a moot point, at least in this town) that strategy has not led technology, but that technology has led strategy. What sort of human intentionality is that? In the case of MIRV, in the absence of any arms control, technology defeated the very rational calculations and wishes of policy makers. We have been worrying about the influence of weapons on wars. Perhaps we should worry a little bit about the influence of weapons on the men who start wars.

On the Origins of the Arms Race Paradigm

Patrick Glynn's essay, "The Sarajevo Fallacy," is remarkable, not only for the argument it makes, but for what it sets out to do. Most discussion of public policy consists of simply taking a position on one or more headline issues of the moment. For instance, the uprising on the West Bank—which fills the news as I write but will probably require an effort of recollection when these lines are read—what should be done about it? The problem is that those headline issues keep changing. As issues disappear from the headlines, whatever we grasped about the world through a particular case disappears from our minds. So as you and I take positions and read other people's positions from issue to issue, it becomes a labor of Sisyphus. There is normally no learning in public policy discourse.

Patrick Glynn has done something quite different. He analyzes a way of thinking that underlies repeated positions that people have taken on various headline issues over the last ninety years or so, a way of thinking that has powerfully determined policy without our being aware of it. His focus is the belief that wars are caused by arms races, or, more broadly, by unintentional, impersonal processes, such as the action-reaction arms race model, the cult of the offensive, the bureaucratic politics of military mobilization plans, misperceptions, militarism—there is a whole series of them. And he calls this the arms race paradigm.

Patrick Glynn is quite right that this paradigm was a view that did not exist through most of the thousands of years in which there existed weapons and wars and the outbreaks of wars. The older belief, the more naive belief, was that wars usually break out because one side or both sides want to start a war. I say usually, not in all cases, because it was always admitted that wars can sometimes start by mistake or even by action and reaction. When the first thematic attacks on large defense efforts appeared in the nineteenth century, the argument was not on the grounds that such efforts might cause a war or provoke an overreaction on the other side but simply on the grounds that they cost too much. That was the position of British radical reform politicians Richard Cobden and John Bright, for example, in arguing against large naval expenditures in the middle of the nineteenth century. So the arms race paradigm is a new mental category in human history.

Where does it come from? This ought to be an important focus of intellectual history. Unless we can answer this question, we won't know why we believe what we do believe about war and peace. Let me use an example to show why the historical question is important for current policy debate. For a long time, the concept of totalitarianism played a role in organizing thinking about the nature of the Soviet and Chinese political systems similar to the role of the arms race paradigm in organizing our thinking about war and peace. It happens that the origins of the concept of totalitarianism are known: it was first used by Mussolini and his opponents in the twenties to describe the distinctive character of Italian fascism and then by political scientists to describe Nazi Germany, Fascist Italy, and Stalin's Soviet Union. Thus, when the adequacy of the totalitarian model of Soviet and Chinese politics began to be questioned, everyone could see how the question should be argued: by discussing the extent to which the contemporary Soviet Union and China resembled, and differed from, Fascist Italy, Nazi Germany, and Stalin's Soviet Union. Because we knew when the concept of totalitarianism originated, we could identify the experience it responded to and begin to think how this experience might be different from our own. With the arms race paradigm, we lack even this starting point for discussing the concept. There is no book or dissertation devoted to the origin of the arms race paradigm.[1] So where do we begin?

Perhaps we can now begin with the work of Glynn, who is, I believe, the first person to try in print to establish the origins of the arms race paradigm. He argues that the arms race paradigm comes from the experience of World War I. I believe this is absolutely correct and that it is a key insight about arms races and arms control. In our lifetimes, we are used to experiencing rapid changes in the intellectual-cultural climate of public policy. Viewed from the distance of the late 1980s, for example, the 1960s seem almost as far away as the Victorian age. The clothes, the songs, the colors, the styles of art, the vision of America and the world—all were quite different. But the assumptions about arms races that appear in the debate over SDI are identical to those that figured in the ABM debate of 1969 to 1970. In fact, as Glynn argues, we can dig back to the period just after World War I and find the very same assumptions current. By the end of World War I, those assumptions had also become authoritative: while there were always Colonel Blimps who disregarded the arms race paradigm, there was no one in the aftermath of World War I who explicitly challenged it. It was as a result of World War I that the arms race paradigm became an establishment view. Patrick Glynn has made the past live again; and by doing that, he has freed us from that past, which was working in our minds without our being aware of it.

I do have a certain nuance of difference with Glynn about the origins of the arms race paradigm, but it's a footnote. Glynn admits that the arms race paradigm originated, not in response to the war, but in the decades before it. The way I would formulate this thought is to say that the arms race paradigm was a minority view before World War I; the war converted it into an establishment view. That leaves us with the question of just when the arms race paradigm originated and why. Even though the answer clearly lies at some point within the fifty years preceding 1914, it remains important to reach a precise answer. Only when we know why human beings began to feel a need for the concept *arms race* (and the rest of the arms race paradigm), when they had felt no need for it over the previous thousands of years, will we understand whether we ourselves need that concept.

Glynn ultimately traces the arms race paradigm to the liberal-democratic vision of politics, which blames war, not on aggressive states, but somehow on the nature of politics. He could have added there, I think, that it is a common view in democratic society that impersonal forces, rather than individual intentions, determine events. That position was argued with wonderful elegance by Alexis de Tocqueville in the chapter of *Democracy in America* on the characteristics of historians in democratic societies, where he says that in aristocratic societies people tend to believe in a "great man theory" of history,[2] a theory that overrated the power of the individual over events. In democratic societies, people, who are atoms, who are lost in the vast indeterminate ocean of a society, mobile and rootless, tend to think that events and individuals' destinies are determined by broad, long-term, impersonal forces. Marxism, economic determinism, and the arms race are obviously versions of that point of view, which is peculiarly congenial to democratic societies.

In reexamining the experience that produced the arms race paradigm, Glynn appropriately concentrates on the naval arms race before World War I. Using the Fischer school of historians of German domestic politics, he shows that the naval build-up was not a matter of action-reaction but an explicit effort to challenge Britain and to overthrow the existing international order. Bismarck's successors' attempt to overthrow the international order crafted thirty years before, an act that displays vividly the restlessness of Germany's rulers, was a momentous turn in European history.

It must be admitted that the Germans did fear the English, as the arms race paradigm predicts. They feared a Copenhagen, in which their fleet would suddenly be destroyed one sunny morning. How does Glynn account for this fear? Following Jonathan Steinberg, he argues that the Germans really were afraid, but they were afraid of what the British would do if they found out what the Germans were up to. He calls that peculiar kind of fear *strategic fear*. I think that's an important distinction and an important elucidation of Soviet behavior: the Soviets have probably been afraid of us during episodes such as Andropov's campaign against the Euromissile deployment; I don't completely dismiss that. But I believe a large part of their fear has been what we would do if we found out what was in the back of their minds.

Glynn traces German strategic fear to social Darwinism, which "nowhere else...[became] so central to national thought and feeling as in Germany." He argues that only by ignoring the intellectual environment that surrounded and conditioned all policymaking and crisis management before World War I can one put impersonal processes, such as the arms race, in their place. Here Glynn and the historians of Germany he follows, such as the Fischer school and Jonathan Steinberg, are entirely convincing. Glynn is unquestionably right that these intellectual currents were stronger in Germany than anywhere else. But it seems to me that at this point Glynn does not follow through with his intention of expounding the distinctiveness of German attitudes. Before World War I, social Darwinism was a phenomenon throughout the West. Thus, to explain German political ambitions in terms of social Darwinism is in a sense to assimilate them to the familiar. What Glynn omits is the growing intellectual influence of Friedrich Nietzsche in Germany after 1890. The element that Nietzsche added to the exaltation of competition and strife in social Darwinism was the explicit attack on morality. Nietzsche had announced that God is dead and that all *values*, a term he popularized, are merely arbitrary creations of the human will. These doctrines were in themselves certain to undermine traditional restraints on war, domination, and exploitation, especially where the political culture was warlike to begin with. But Nietzsche drew the lesson himself, writing that a good war justifies any cause. To understand what was distinctive about the German intellectual climate, we need to ponder the impact of statements such as the following,

> ...life itself is essentially appropriation, injury, overpowering of what is alien and weaker, suppression, hardness, imposition of one's own forms, incorporation and at least, at its mildest, exploitation....[3]

During the period from the middle of the 1890s up to the outbreak of the war, this very radical teaching became widely known and admired by the German academic establishment, by men such as Max Weber. This academic establishment legitimized German imperialism and the creation of a great German navy. The years of the rapid growth of Nietzsche's influence in Germany were the very years of the momentous turn by Germany from the Bismarckian order to *Weltpolitik.*

Strategic fear can be seen in Wilhelmine Germany and in the USSR, but I am less sure about the wider comparison of the Soviet Union and of Imperial Germany that seems implicit in Glynn's argument. This analogy is certainly more accurate than the widespread notion that the Soviet Union is basically like the West in its international conduct, so that the relationship between the two sides can be seen as determined by impersonal, interactive processes. But there are great differences between German and Soviet behavior in both directions: Soviet conduct is better in some ways, worse in others. On the one hand, the relationship between Germany and Britain was much more normal: their citizens traveled freely back and forth, read each other's books, traded freely, lived under a monarch and a parliament. Soviet tactics have tended to be more ruthless, as in Soviet support for terrorism. But, on the other hand, the Soviet Union has never chosen to push an international crisis into general war, as Glynn argues Germany did in July 1914. We may have been lucky, or Soviet behavior may reflect the absence of the explosive German combination of ambition and fear symbolized by the slogan "world power or downfall." I hope that Glynn will elaborate this comparison further as he completes his work on arms control. Because his present essay deals with the origins of the arms race paradigm, he has no real opportunity to interpret Soviet conduct.

My only misgiving about the argument is whether Glynn goes far enough in criticizing the arms race paradigm. In many places, he seems to use language drawn from that paradigm. He speaks of "the vast increase in the size of national arsenals," of programs that "seemed continually to react upon one another," of an "escalating arms race," of "an all-out arms race," of the "generalized arms race." There are a number of phrases such as "spiraling costs" and "the direction of the action-reaction pattern."[4] Let me quote one additional reference: "Specific actions on the part of the British...generally were followed by comparable steps on the part of Germany."[5] Glynn is surely aware that this entire language comes from the arms race paradigm. Some of this language may be a product of the mode of exposition, but it seems that Glynn has a certain tendency to couple the criticism of the arms race paradigm with the notion that it was going on anyway, but that Germany was driving it. Glynn seems to imply that the kind of tension in the relationship between the arms of the two sides was what the post-1919 model has described.

At one point Glynn concludes, "Indeed, most of the lessons that the revisionists applied to all the powers...in truth pertained decisively only to Germany." Is this possible? Can the language and many of the concepts of the arms race paradigm, which was apparently invented to deny the responsibility of particular nations, be maintained when responsibility for the disturbance of the international order is plausibly attached to one nation? This is a conceptual issue I cannot discuss here. But it does seem to me that Glynn follows the basic language and concepts of the arms race paradigm more than the facts require.

In the limited space available, I can do no more than refer to what I have written elsewhere. The table below shows German and British construction of battleships and battle cruisers from just before the German Navy Law of 1898 to 1914.

These figures do not show an "escalating" or an "all-out" arms race, nor a general action-reaction pattern. There was no British reply to the German 50 percent increase in building under the 1906 amendment, nor a German response to the vast British increase in 1909.

There were some very limited, but violent, action-reaction interactions during the period between 1905 and 1909, and I think our belief that there was something called an arms race is a generalization of those limited events, which I would argue were very fortuitous, very much conditioned by the particular circumstances.

I suspect that the event that touched off the violent interactions was the building of the much more powerful *Dreadnought* and *Invincible* classes of capital ships in 1905. As Jon Tesuro Sumida shows in his book *In Defense of Naval Supremacy*,[7] the dreadnought and invincible revolutions were in no way a response to anything Germany had done, but reproduced British Admiral Fisher's much

Table 1 German and British Authorizations of Battleships
and Battle Cruisers[6]

Year	Germany	Britain
1896	1	5
1897	1	4
1898	2	7
1899	3	2
1900	2	2
1901	2	3
1902	2	2
1903	2	4[a]
1904	2	2
1905	2	4[b]
1906	2[b]	3
1907	3	3
1908	4	2
1909	4	10[c]
1910	4	7
1911	4	5
1912	2	5[d]
1913	3	5
1914	2	4

[a]*Includes two ships purchased for diplomatic reasons.*
[b]*All ships authorized after 1904 in Britain and after 1905 in Germany are dreadnoughts.*
[c]*Includes one Australian ship and one ship paid for by New Zealand.*
[d]*Includes one ship paid for by the Malay states.*

earlier vision of the best possible warship, a vision shaped by the
strategic situation in which Britain faced the French and Russian
navies.

The dreadnought revolution in turn triggered changes in
German warship design that made the fleet planned in 1898 much
more dangerous to Britain.[8] Most destabilizing of all was the fact
that the *Dreadnought* and *Invincible* made earlier British battleships
and armored cruisers (the pre-dreadnoughts) almost instantly out-
moded. It was this fact that gave the young German Navy a chance
against Britain commensurate with its ultimate ambitions.

Other fortuitous circumstances also conditioned the dramatic
action-action dynamics of 1905-1909. As I have written elsewhere,

The Germans were impelled forward by the pattern of their 1900
Navy Law, which had been engineered by Admiral Tirpitz to create

a methodical pattern of shipbuilding, year after year, to reassure the Reichstag. At the same time, though, the Navy Law stipulated that more ships be built in the early years of the program than in the later years. The hope of Tirpitz was that, when the annual building rate was due to decline, a way would be found to continue building at the pace of the earlier years. The year of the Dreadnought, 1905, was also the year in which the German building program called for a drop from three new ships to two; the Germans thus faced the choice of accepting a thirty-three percent decline in shipbuilding or of augmenting their plans by fifty percent. If Germany followed the British move to the Dreadnought type, the fifty percent rise in programmed forces would consist of ships far bigger and more threatening to Britain—just at the moment when Britain's immense lead in pre-Dreadnoughts was vanishing.[9]

Glynn has opened up for us the possibility of asking the question: Are we, when we speak of arms races, attributing to the whole of history something that happened during four or five years before World War I? I think so, but I would be more radical. I would say the whole concept of the arms race is a fallacious concept—not that it has no truth, but that it has a very limited, narrow truth—that has, on some limited occasions, been made into a master concept.

This brings me to my last point. Glynn's most important argument for policy purposes is that the arms race paradigm weakens the commitment to deterrence. Looking at history as he has done, I think there can be no doubt that this is true. Glynn poses an important intellectual and moral problem for defenders of the arms race paradigm. I wonder, however, whether there was the latent implication that deterrence would be strong, or could be strong, if it weren't weakened by the arms race paradigm. There is a suggestion that Glynn shares the view, which I think Ronald Reagan once quoted: *Qui vis pacem para bellum* ("Let him who desires peace prepare for war"). Now deterrence has two senses. One is the technical sense that was discovered by Albert Wohlstetter in the early 1950s—in Herman Kahn's definition, the capacity to inflict unacceptable damage in a second strike after being struck. Deterrence in this sense has proved sturdy since the 1950s. But it is delicate: it depends on the precise technical characteristics of weapons and continuous force modernization.

Another, more vague sense of deterrence is simply the possession of a preponderance of force. I suspect that deterrence in this sense is useful, but not very powerful, in preventing war. After all, the Central Powers, if you look at the money and men available, were somewhat weaker than the Franco-Russian alliance plus England. The Entente powers outweighed Germany and Austria-Hungary in most categories of national power, including manpower, money (given the position of London and Paris as international financial centers), money spent on defense (£222 million to £147 million by A.J.P. Taylor's figures[10]), most categories of industrial production, soldiers under arms, and naval strength. And the Germans clearly understood that England was on the other side, even if they didn't understand that England would be at war. They also knew that the Italians were not eager to fight at their side. Why weren't the Germans deterred? I think German social Darwinism was not altogether wrong. German society had a vitality, a thrust and drive, that they thought would compensate for a balance of power that was not particularly favorable. And they were almost right.

That points out that the axiom, if you want peace prepare for war, is the other side of the arms race paradigm. The arms race paradigm says that wars happen because of having weapons; the above axiom says that wars happen because of not having enough weapons. Both of them imply a kind of dethroning of politics and of culture as causes of war. I'm not sure that Glynn has criticized the two sides of that coin with equal force.

The final lesson of this very powerful essay is that one has to discard mechanistic understandings of how wars start and return to trying to reintegrate war intellectually into the broader horizon of politics and culture. We do not know where this quest will end, because we are excavating layers of doctrine that have accumulated for the last century and hidden the genuine experience of war and peace. If, however, I were to hazard a guess about the outcome of that quest, I venture that it will be not a confidence in our ability to prevent wars, which I think sometimes seems to emerge from Glynn's essay, but unease and a certain sense of tragedy.

Notes

[1] This will be the subject of one chapter in the book I am preparing on arms races.

[2] Alexis De Tocqueville, "Some Characteristics Peculiar to Historians in Democratic Centuries," *Democracy in America*, Vol. II, J.P. Mayer, ed., George Lawrence, trans. (Garden City: Anchor Books, Doubleday and Co., Inc., 1969), 493–97.

[3] Friedrich Nietzsche, *Aphorism 259, Beyond Good and Evil* (New York: Vintage Books, 1966), 203.

[4] Patrick Glynn, "The Sarajevo Fallacy: The Historical and Intellectual Origins of Arms Control Theology," *The National Interest* (Fall 1987): 6, 10, 15, 17, 18.

[5] Ibid., 13.

[6] Charles H. Fairbanks, Jr., "Arms Races: The Metaphor and the Facts," *The National Interest* (Fall 1985): 77.

[7] Jon T. Sumida, *In Defense of Naval Supremacy: Financial Limitation, Technological Innovation, and British Naval Policy, 1899–1914* (Winchester, Mass.: Unwin Hyman, Inc., 1989).

[8] Charles H. Fairbanks, Jr., "Choosing Among Technologies in the Anglo-German Naval Arms Competition, 1898–1915," *Naval History: The Seventh Symposium of the U.S. Naval Academy*, William Cogar, ed. (Wilmington: Scholarly Resources, 1988).

[9] Fairbanks, "Arms Races," 82–83.

[10] A.J.P. Taylor, *The Struggle for Mastery in Europe, 1848–1918* (London: Oxford University Press, 1971), xxviii.

J. DAVID SINGER

On the Danger of Single-Case Analogies

Let me begin by observing that every historical analogy is falla-cious. That is, since no two cases are identical, no single case can serve as a reliable guide to contemporary policy. We must, of course, go further and note that any useful lessons from history need to rest on the observation of all the relevant cases—or, at least, a credibly representative sample. Doing that, we can then safely generalize, for example, that in such a fraction of the cases, such-and-such a behavior pattern culminated in such-and-such an out-come. While a large number of such solid generalizations will not guarantee success in policy, they can appreciably reduce our error rate.

In addition to the main theme in "The Sarajevo Fallacy," Glynn makes a second, and equally interesting, argument. That is, we must be careful not to generalize from a single case or episode and to avoid drawing erroneous inferences from either a single case or a population of cases. We must, he suggests, properly understand and interpret each historical case—a charming, but not particularly helpful suggestion, since he offers no criteria for ascer-taining which interpretation is the correct and proper one. To be more specific, neither he nor any single-case analyst tells us what rules are used to arrive at the particular rendering of the case; to serve as a prudent guide, these rules must be so clear and explicit that other analysts can confidently apply them to the same case and arrive at the same conclusions.

Let me illustrate. Building on the work of Fritz Fischer, our author concludes that the war "was the product of a deliberate bid by the German leadership for European domination." This sort of assertion leads to two serious problems. First, what substantiated evidence is adduced? All that we have here are the selected actions and quotations of a few observers and the omission of other events and interpretations that might weaken the explanation being proffered. One might, with equal plausibility, offer a different interpretation of the onset of World War I. Rather than lay it largely at the Kaiser's doorstep, let us consider a more complex model, shaped by past circumstances as well as the goals and motives of the European allies.

To begin, there was a mood in most of Europe that was far from pacifist. From London to Petrograd, and certainly including France, Germany, and Austria, there existed a mix of late Victorian disenchantment, cultural stultification, and indifferent economic conditions on the one hand, and a rather romantic view of war (thanks largely to the neat and tidy Franco-Prussian War) on the other. The result was not war fever, but a certain sense of attraction to that sort of adventure. Then there were the French, Russian, and German war plans, all of which rested to some extent on the advantage of fast mobilization and striking first. While the Schlieffen plan was clearly the most ambitious and bold, the Germans were not the only ones poised for preemption and confident in their capabilities. With the Russian decision to support the Serbs, Germany's only real ally (Austria) was suddenly in great jeopardy from the growing and modernizing forces of the Tsar. Under such circumstances, it is small wonder that the Kaiser and his circle—already intrigued by, but not committed to, imperialist dreams—on hearing from the General Staff that delay would be fatal both to Austria and to Germany itself, would agree to the strike through Belgium. Obviously, the story is more complicated, especially in light of the ability to avoid war in the Bosnian crisis earlier, but it certainly is not as simple as Glynn would have us believe. Nor, I would urge, is the onset of any major war of the past two centuries.

If it is problematic to insist on such idiosyncratic interpretations of a given historical case, it is highly imprudent to draw any sort of generalizations from those specific interpretations, especially if those interpretations are to be a basis for national policy. Take, for example, the notion that the Sarajevo incident would never have escalated to war in the absence of the alliance commitments of the Allies and the Central Powers; that is, the war was caused by these alliance bonds. Thus, major power elites knew to steer clear of such entanglements in the 1920 to 1940 period, only to discover that a strong alliance among the Allies would have deterred Hitler's Germany. And, having learned that lesson, they went about alliance-building with a passion in the wake of World War II, probably aggravating and prolonging the Cold War well beyond what it might have been. A similar set of inconsistent lessons could be drawn from the excessively punctual mobilizations in 1914 and the tardy ones of 1938 to 1939.

Having expressed my initial skepticism of policy-relevant lessons that are drawn from a single case in an idiosyncratic and nonreproducible fashion, let me turn to some of the more dubious ones that are found in Glynn's article. Perhaps the most sweeping conclusion is that war arises out of conscious and relatively rational choice. This statement is true in the trivial sense that policy choices are constantly being made by national security elites, but it ignores the extraordinary constraints on those choices and the degree of rationality that obtains as they are being made. Regarding the latter, we must never forget that policy makers are always playing several roles in several different games. Certainly they think about their nation's physical security, but they also give an impressive amount of attention to their own welfare and that of their constituencies at home and even abroad. They worry about looking too dovish or too hawkish in the eyes of colleagues, opinion makers, reference figures, and close friends (including spouses and children); deviance can be costly to career, clout, and self-image. And they also give more than passing consideration to the welfare of their bureau, agency, domestic allies, and political cronies. Every national government is a relatively loose (and often unstable) coalition of individuals, agencies, and interest groups, all of whom are pursuing multiple goals, of which national security is but one.

Combined with this ambiguous set of priorities is a second and related constraint on rationality: the relative absence of hard evidence. That is, the sort of systematic research that will eventually produce greater confidence that a given policy under given conditions will lead to a given outcome just has not yet been done. Thus, when confronted with a policy decision, with several equally plausible options and little or no compelling knowledge as to results, we tend to go with the one that is most professionally and personally satisfactory.

Regardless of the extent to which rational choice is mitigated by these factors of ignorance, psychic need, and internal politics, it is essential that we recognize the constraints imposed by the past. The state of the regional system, the types and capabilities of the relevant national regimes, and the trade, military, and diplomatic configurations are all inherited from prior conditions, events, and decisions. Thus, we need not be surprised at the frequency with which we hear statements to the effect that we had no choice.

Let me now turn to another dominant theme: that arms and their accumulation are not culpable when it comes to the onset of war; as the cliché has it, weapons don't make war, men make war. I submit that it takes both—neither is sufficient by itself. Consider what I would call the *deterrence-to-provocation ratio*, in which it is understood that certain levels and types of weaponry and personnel serve to inhibit and deter expansionistic tendencies on the part of would-be aggressors. But beyond such levels, deployments, and so on, the effect is more alarming and provocative than reassuring and restraining; obviously, the line of demarcation is vague, shifting, and difficult to measure. But a failure to appreciate that such a line (or zone) exists is to invite reciprocity, mutual escalation, and a psycho-political process that plays into the hands of the over-armers on both or all sides. In that process, we not only get more preparedness than is good for national security; we also get an incremental increase in the economic and political power of those with a touching faith in the military instrument, accompanied by a decrease in the role of those with a more prudent and pragmatic turn of mind. In other words, men may decide to make weapons, but in so doing they initiate a process that all too often is one in which the men and the weapons interact to make war.

In sum, both the historical detail and the rhetorical flair that characterize Glynn's paper are impressive, but, in the end, its flaws are close to disabling. First, there are too many equally plausible but appreciably different interpretations of the conditions and events that account for the onset of World War I. Second, even if the interpretation at hand were persuasive beyond mere anecdotal plausibility, we have no reason to believe that an examination of the nearly one thousand other confrontations since 1816 would support Glynn's more general interpretation of how they escalate to war. Third, the author goes well beyond the acceptable when he urges that we base our national security policies on an empirical base of such fragility. With so much at stake, we need to do considerably better.

HARRY G. SUMMERS, JR.

On the Relevance of Public Opinion

Commenting on the "distaste of [British] Foreign Office officials for the task of accounting for policy to an uninformed and emotional public," Glynn concludes that "the failure of Britain to respond effectively [to the Sarajevo crisis] was in no small part due to a failure to adapt foreign policy to the exigencies of democratic rule, to shape a public mandate for policy essential to Britain's long-range survival and prosperity." As he goes on to say, "This problem is one that the present-day democracies have by no means entirely solved."[1]

Not only have "present-day democracies" (the United States in particular) failed to solve the problem, but also their lack of an appreciation for the critical importance of public support has become even more pronounced in the latter half of the twentieth century.

In the first half of this century, President Woodrow Wilson and President Franklin Roosevelt went beyond their presidential powers to support the Allies in the First and Second World Wars. But neither dared send troops into extended combat without a declaration of war from the Congress as mandated by Article I of the Constitution, and neither had the chutzpah to claim, as did Presidents Lyndon Johnson and Richard Nixon, that their appointment as Commander-in-Chief of the armed forces granted by Article II of the Constitution gave them the authority to independently wage protracted war.[2]

That hubris—first displayed by President Harry S Truman in June 1950 when he committed American troops to war (what he labeled a police action) in Korea without first seeking a declaration of war from the Congress—grew out of America's Cold War confrontation with the Soviet Union and its communist allies. The American foreign policy elite, in and out of government, began to mirror their adversaries, and they became a kind of "vanguard of the proletariat" who knew best what was good for the American people.

In words that would have made the pre-World War I British Foreign Office proud, Professor Robert Osgood stated in his influential 1957 book, *Limited War,* that even though the American people, because of their national traditions and ideology, would be hostile to the kind of strategy he proposed, that strategy must still be adopted.[3] What made Osgood's approach so appealing—and what ultimately made it so disastrous—was that by eliminating the war-peace threshold, it short-circuited the systems of checks and balances that the framers of the Constitution had deliberately enacted to control American foreign and military policy.

Although not as well known as the nuclear threshold, the war-peace threshold is a critical aspect of American military policy. Whereas the nuclear threshold is the divide between conventional and nuclear war, the war-peace threshold is the divide between the peacetime use of military forces and their commitment to sustained combat abroad.[4]

It is a divide the American people have always been reluctant to cross, and for most of our history, this dividing line was scrupulously observed. But after World War II, theorists replaced *peace* with *cold war* (defined as a power struggle between contending nations, as if that were something new in the history of the world) and the war-peace threshold was dismissed as an anachronism. The distinction was now between *cold war* and *limited war* where, as the Army's 1962 doctrinal manual stated, "the dividing line…is neither distinct nor absolute."[5]

But while theorists may have had difficulty discerning that dividing line, it was all too apparent to the American people. As President Johnson ultimately discovered after he crossed the war-peace threshold in 1965 and sent American troops into action in Vietnam, committing American combat troops and losing Americans on the battlefield is war, no matter what the theorists choose to call it. But it took a quarter-century and the debacle in Vietnam before the war-peace threshold was rediscovered.

In a speech to the National Press Club on November 28, 1984, then-Secretary of Defense Caspar W. Weinberger laid out what later became known as the "Weinberger Doctrine" regarding the use of U.S. military force abroad. "I believe the post-war period has taught us several lessons," he said, "and from them I have developed six major tests to be applied when we are weighing the use of U.S. combat forces abroad."

Among these tests—the focus on vital interests, the commitment to win, the need for clear-cut objectives, the need to keep objectives and force levels in balance, and the admonition to use military force only as a last resort—was the requirement that "before the U.S. commits combat forces abroad, there must be some reasonable assurance we will have the support of the American people and their elected representatives in the Congress." Secretary Weinberger went on to say, "This support cannot be achieved unless we are candid in making clear the threats we face; the support cannot be sustained without continuing and close consultation. We cannot fight a battle with the Congress at home while asking our troops to win overseas."[6]

Although all of his preconditions were important, the need for public and congressional support was paramount. Not only did his formulation reestablish the war-peace threshold, it also reestablished the theoretical basis for American military strategy. As the preeminent military theorist Carl von Clausewitz pointed out over 150 years ago,

> The only source of war is politics—the intercourse of governments and peoples; but it is apt to be assumed that war suspends that intercourse and replaces it by a wholly different condition, ruled by no law but its own.... We maintain, on the contrary, that war is simply a continuation of political intercourse, with the addition of other means.

"If that is so," he emphasizes, "then war cannot be divorced from political life, and whenever this occurs in our thinking about war, the many links that connect the two elements are destroyed and we are left with something pointless and devoid of sense."[7]

Most revealing is the fact that the call for public and congressional support proved to be the most controversial aspect of Secretary Weinberger's remarks. This fact revealed a basic error that has plagued American strategy for over a generation—we had unwittingly cut ourselves off from our political-military roots and in so doing had been left, as Clausewitz warned, with "something pointless and devoid of sense."

For most of our history, the war-peace threshold—the need for public and congressional support to both legitimize crossing that threshold and then to sustain subsequent wartime military operations—was taken as gospel. This threshold was considered so fundamental by the framers of the Constitution (particularly the twenty-three who were soldiers in the Revolutionary War) that they wrote it into the Constitution—specifically in the requirement that only Congress (the periodically elected representatives of the people) could declare war. The framers thus sought to ensure that the government, the people, and the military would act in concert.

In his masterwork, *On War*, written almost fifty years after the American Constitution was adopted, Clausewitz provided a theoretical basis for those common sense constitutional prescriptions. Having learned from the French Revolution what America had discovered in its own revolution, Clausewitz noted the critical importance of what he called the "remarkable trinity" of the government, the people, and the army.

The government provided the direction and the military the instrument, but the passions of the people provided the very engine of war. "A theory that ignores any one of them or seeks to fix an arbitrary relationship between them," he warned, "would conflict with reality to such an extent that for this reason alone it would be totally useless."[8]

By the 1980s, however, these prescriptions and warnings had long since been forgotten, and Weinberger's reaffirmation was ridiculed and belittled. Critics from both the Right and the Left heaped scorn on his insistence that the American people and their congressional representatives should determine questions of war and peace.

But for moral as well as practical reasons, the critics were dead wrong. Morally, as the Constitution sought to ensure, the American people, from whose ranks soldiers would be drawn to risk their lives on the battlefield, ought to have some say in the matter. And for practical reasons, if congressional support is not assured, who will pay for the war?

Secretary Weinberger's efforts notwithstanding, U.S. policy makers are still as reluctant as their British Foreign Office predecessors to "account for policy to an uninformed and emotional public." But Vietnam and, more recently, the Iran-Contra fiasco, are evidence that, unless they do so, their policies will inevitably fail.

Notes

[1]Patrick Glynn, "The Sarajevo Fallacy: The Historical and Intellectual Origins of Arms Control Theology," *The National Interest* No. 9 (Fall 1987): 29.

[2]Ninety-first Congress, 2d Sess., Committee on Foreign Relations, United States Senate, *Termination of the Middle East and South East Asian Resolutions, Report to Accompany Senate Concurrent Resolution 64, May 15, 1970* (Washington, D.C.: U.S. Government Printing Office, 1970), 7.

[3]Robert Osgood, *Limited War*, quoted in Stephen Peter Rosen's "Vietnam and the American Theory of Limited War," *International Security* (Fall 1982): 85.

[4]For a more detailed discussion of the war-peace threshold see my *Sound Military Decisions* (forthcoming).

[5]*Field Manual 100-5, Field Service Regulations: Operations* (Washington, D.C.: Department of the Army, February 1962), 4–5.

[6]Caspar W. Weinberger, "The Uses of Military Power," *Department of Defense News Release No. 609-64* (Washington, D.C.: Office of the Assistant Secretary of Defense, Public Affairs, November 28, 1984), 5–6.

[7]Carl von Clausewitz, *On War* (Princeton: Princeton University Press, 1976), 605.

[8]Ibid., 89.

PART III

Proceedings from the Public Workshop

The Meaning of Sarajevo in 1988

PATRICK GLYNN: Each commentator has made very interesting comments on my article. As is evident from their remarks, we could approach the article from two directions: by discussing the theoretical issues that the article raises about war or by discussing the more timely kinds of policy issues about arms control. Perhaps we'll try both.

First, let me focus on the comment that I liked the best, even though I disagree. I am referring to Charles Fairbanks's point about the degree to which arms races are interactive and the degree to which faith in deterrence is, in a certain sense, the other side of the arms race paradigm.

Fairbanks and I have talked before, and we differ on the following questions, the answers to which I think are ultimately a bit technical: To what degree were the British watching the Germans, and the Germans watching the British, and the Germans watching the French, in the period leading up to 1914? My sense is that the period was fairly interactive. When a nation accumulates military power, what it is concerned with is the comparative relation between its power and the other nations'. By nature, the accumulation of military power is an interactive process. Look, for example, at what the Germans were doing: they were watching British developments very closely, they were watching French developments very closely, and they were watching Russian developments very closely. I believe that's happened between the United States and the Soviet Union, too. Sometimes we have been in error, as was true in the 1950s when Soviet strategic deception convinced the political leadership that there was a bomber gap and then convinced the larger polity that there was a missile gap. My sense is that the processes are interactive.

However, the more profound issue that Fairbanks raises, which is somewhat troubling, is the question of whether deterrence is a major way, or foolproof way, or comparatively foolproof way, of preventing war. I am not prepared entirely to dismiss either his explanation of German behavior in 1914 or his pessimism. I tried in the article, I thought, to point generally in the direction that policy makers could have taken to prevent the war, but I tried not to say definitely that they could have prevented the war.

I think Fairbanks is right in saying that the Germans were willing to attack even if the odds on paper seemed against them. It seems to me that the calculation of the possibility of a military victory, which was based...on a fairly close analysis of French and Russian capabilities, was a *sine qua non* of being able to persuade the political leadership to push forward with the escalation of the crisis. What I have tried to suggest is that deterrence is not simply a matter of having military forces, although it clearly is largely that. Deterrence is also a matter of being able to translate those military forces into a political power factor at a given moment. Two elements were critical in 1914: one was the tenuousness of the Entente, which is in contrast to the relative firmness of NATO (even today, despite the problems). That is, the Germans had a very good shot at splitting the Entente because, as the Russian Foreign Minister said, it was like the sea monster—nobody knew whether this alliance existed or not.

The other element of the political power factor was that irresolute British policy in that critical period of time gave the German general staff the sense that the British would not be involved, and thus British interference would not be a problem.

So it seems that one cannot say with certainty—this is all hypothesis—that war could have been prevented. But at the same time, Lloyd George's Mansion House speech in 1911 was a very bellicose statement (coming from the British), which changed Germany's attitude toward the war overnight. I'm not as pessimistic as Fairbanks about the ability to deter war, even in 1911, and I'm certainly not pessimistic now. I do think that a credible scenario was indispensable to the aggression, and there were ways of making that scenario less credible. There was a mechanism by which deterrence could have operated.

J. David Singer raises the question whether all of these generalizations are futile, which reminds me, if I can draw on my literary background, of a statement in an essay by T.S. Eliot about Shakespeare. Eliot said that Shakespeare got more essential history from reading Plutarch than most men could get from a lifetime in the British Museum.

It seems to me that the effort to accumulate and analyze successive instances of similar events is the intellectual equivalent of throwing money at a problem. Because of the way that politics works, it is essential to have a deeper human understanding of what is going on. Maybe my literary background prejudices me, but I would also say my limited experience as a policy maker—as someone participating in that process—also prejudices me in this direction. One can come to intuitive political judgments that work. Furthermore, political policy makers have to make those judgments. We can't wait for the study of the thousand correlates of war. On the other side, the people who are compiling the numbers have suppositions that they are perhaps less likely to acknowledge simply because they have opted for a quantitative framework. A good example is the Holsti-North study, which gave credence to the notion that the First World War was an accident. These researchers took documents, divided them mechanically and numerically into perceptions, categorized them, did the equivalent of computer sorting, and came up with a totally incorrect explanation of what had occurred.

I think Singer and I have a fundamental difference, but it is dictated both by epistemological considerations (that is, I don't think you can get at these issues quantitatively), and by practical considerations. Policy makers must have rules of thumb to interact. They are faced with decisions every day. They have a defense program. They must have approximations of reality. The closer those approximations get, the better the policy is going to be.

When it comes to the practicality issue, I agree with the point that Harry Summers made about political support of the populist policy. I think this is something we all know. It is interesting to note the degree to which British policy suffered in 1914 from a kind of Foreign Office snottiness in addition to liberal-democratic ambivalence. They just did not like the idea of having to explain their reasoning to the people. Crowe, the Foreign Office Senior Clerk, was brilliant. He understood exactly what the Germans were doing, but nobody in the general populace ever understood what was going on. The whole crisis occurred with most of Europe playing tennis, or whatever the people were doing. Hence public awareness is a very important part of policy.

Finally, to flip over from the kind of theoretical issues of war to the more practical issue of arms control, I want to add just one remark about Leon Wieseltier's comments. I reject the historical characterization of the classical liberal-democratic view as a "caricature." I don't think that what I present is a caricature. In fact, if you read what the radicals were saying about war and peace, their view was a sort of self-caricature. They were unbelievably naive; in fact, they acknowledged that in 1914 when the war broke out. Many of them repudiated what they believed, but, of course, it was just a matter of time before they reverted to type.

My point is not that this simplistic view is the mind-set of everyone who is interested in arms control. I would never argue that. Rather, I do argue that the notion that one can engage in negotiations and succeed both in stabilizing force configurations and in affecting the course of events is simply wrong. I think the experience of arms control has proved it.

We've been trying for twenty years to get the Soviets to back off on their first-strike capability and to get these stable force configurations. You can lay it out on paper, and it sounds lovely. It looks like it could be done, but, the fact is, the Soviets will not do it. Even under the Strategic Arms Reduction Talks (START) Agreement, if you look carefully at how their forces are evolving in other channels, through other systems, you'll see the same kind of first-strike capability and dangerous destabilizing weapons that we've been trying to control.

This is not really an observation I make on the basis of historical experience so much as on the basis of personal and practical experience dealing with these people. The key issue is the ultimate political ambition of the state involved. If the state has hegemonic ambitions, it will pursue them. It will pursue them in negotiations and out of negotiations, through its build-up. It will not sacrifice, just as the Germans would not sacrifice, that basic tendency. So you can go on until doomsday erecting these very plausible ways of configuring forces that would be more stabilizing, but if the other power is not interested in stability and the status quo, it will do you no good.

MICHAEL MANDELBAUM: I had an unorthodox response to Glynn's article: I liked it. I agree with the history while I disagree with the implications for policy. So my comments will be an elaboration of that point.

I think the history is right, and it is right to correct the mistake in the image of World War I and Sarajevo, which has a certain currency in the scholarly community. But I think that the effect of the Sarajevo paradigm has been more modest than Glynn implies in his article and states more forthrightly in his remarks.

The fact that the Sarajevo paradigm is an incorrect explanation of World War I does not necessarily mean that some of its tenets are irrelevant to the current period, because nuclear weapons make the current period different from all other periods. For the last twenty-five years, the view in the international relations community has been that there are two models for the outbreak of war: the accidental model, as in the case of Sarajevo, and the deliberate model, as in the case of Munich and World War II. But, in fact, there is only one model. World War I began in basically the same way that World War II did, and for the same reasons. To see it as an accidental war is simply historically incorrect.

Why is this first model so popular? I think that the scholarly community has read the present back into the past. There is an understandable concern, an obsession, with the nuclear period and with nuclear war. It is at least arguably the case that nuclear war could only begin by accident. Those who are concerned about nuclear war—and scholars can't help but be influenced by their own circumstances—look to the past for historical lessons to apply to the present. For that reason, I think we scholars in general have misidentified, misspecified, and misunderstood the outbreak of World War I as a way of trying to say something about our own circumstances.

In fact, I think one of the implications of this analysis is that World War I really does not have very much to teach us. To put it another way, World War I does not have as much to teach us about the present as a good deal of literature on international politics implies.

Now, having said that, I think the implications for policy that Glynn draws are not altogether correct—at least I disagree with them. First, the Sarajevo paradigm, the collection of attitudes that Glynn identifies with a particular interpretation of World War I, and which is a prominent theme in the literature of international politics, has not been very important in actual policy nor in history. I point particularly to a brief interpretation of the outbreak of World War II. The collection of attitudes identified by Glynn was not present: appeasement was not to be understood in terms of the lessons of the revisionists or their interpretation of Sarajevo. Similarly, I think Sarajevo has had relatively little impact on our present policy.

Second, it seems to me that precisely because 1914 is a different world from the post-World War II period, some of the implications of the Sarajevo paradigm that are inapplicable to World War I might actually be relevant to our own time. The general point in the large argument is that nuclear weapons have changed the world, and they have changed it in ways that make some of the principles and some of the attitudes at least arguably relevant in a way that they certainly were not beforehand.

I think Glynn's opening statement was a clear example of that point. He opened by saying that we all agree that nuclear war would be a terrible and unthinkable catastrophe. That is certainly not a statement about war that could have commanded the kind of consensus in the past that it does today. Indeed, when the Germans decided to go to war twice in this century, they did so because they believed—in a way that a reasonable person could believe—that the gains would outweigh the losses. We do not believe that about nuclear war. Nobody believes that now. Therefore we are in a different age, one that makes some of the principles that Glynn identifies at least arguably relevant. That distinction may well make arms control a much more serious and rational proposition than it ever was before.

So let me say a couple of things about arms control. First, one can argue that nuclear weapons are different from all other weapons, that they make plausible the notion of a negotiated military equilibrium between two countries that are nonetheless political adversaries. Because of the special character of nuclear weapons, it may be possible to separate military considerations from political ones in a way that was formerly unthinkable, illogical, and absurd. Certainly, as Glynn notes, such a separation did not happen before World War I. If this is true, then, because of the nature of nuclear weapons, arms control becomes a much more plausible tool of statecraft than it was before World War I.

Second, it seems to me that whatever one may say about arms control and its roots in the misinterpretation of Sarajevo, it has simply not been an important part of the post-war period. Here I'm reemphasizing what Leon Wieseltier said. The negotiations between Britain and Germany before World War I were about central strategic issues, such as the effort to stop the naval race that culminated in the Haldane Mission (which failed, as Glynn notes, because the Germans were demanding a political quid pro quo that was absolutely unacceptable to the British). Arms control negotiations are not about central strategic issues: they're marginal. It is true that we, as a political community, tend to impute great importance to arms control. We tend, in some cases, to be obsessed with it; but that says something about us, not about arms control. The explanation lies in the political sociology of the United States, not in a strategic analysis of Soviet-American relations. The lessons of World War I—the misinterpretation of the outbreak of World War I—do not necessarily bear on arms control, because arms control is a marginal and largely symbolic political exercise.

Having said that, let me discuss two other points that are less central, but where I also have some difficulties and some reservations, which I urge Glynn to revisit.

First is the issue of the relationship between domestic structure and foreign policy. One gets a sense from the brief section that Glynn devotes to it in today's remarks that he wants to argue that democracies are more peaceful and undemocratic countries are more aggressive. There may be something to that, and it is important for us to recognize that conflicts have political content—that in judging conflicts, especially those in which we're involved, we ought to pay attention to the political principle that armaments are acquired to protect or advance, and not pay attention to the armaments themselves. A missile is not merely a missile: an American missile is acquired and deployed for certain political purposes, and a Soviet missile is acquired and deployed for different political purposes. So I certainly would not quarrel with emphasis on domestic differences. However, I think the outbreak of World War I poses some problems in making the argument I think Glynn wants to make, and that one *could* make.

As I'm sure you know, there is a school of scholarship of German policy during the Wilhelmine period, the pioneer of which was Eckart Kehr. Kehr argues that the German fleet and *Weltpolitik* in general (more precisely, that which the other countries found most objectionable and what led to the war) were in fact popular in Germany. This policy was in some sense democratic: not in the sense that it was carried out by a democratically constituted government, but in the sense that this was the one Wilhelmine policy that actually made the Kaiser popular.

Second, if you want to distinguish between democratic England and undemocratic Germany, you have the problem of Russia. Russia was far less democratic than Germany, yet Russia was a member of the democratic coalition.

Third, what the Germans wanted was to have an empire, a middle European empire. They wanted a middle European empire, in part, because the other great powers had empires. The British had their worldwide network of colonies, the United States had expanded across North America in the nineteenth century, and

Russia had done the same thing in the East in the eighteenth and nineteenth centuries. The Germans felt, first of all, that if they did not acquire a comparable empire, they would lose out in the Darwinian competition for power. Second, the Germans felt that they were entitled to an empire. You may have heard the catch word, *Gleichberechtigung*—"equal entitlement." Before World War II, the Germans and Japanese asked, "Why are the British entitled to their empire—and the French, and the Americans, and the Russians—but we aren't?" Well, that's a pretty good question. Whatever one says about that question and about German behavior, I think it's very difficult to correlate this cause of war—which indeed was the central cause of war—with a distinction between democratic and undemocratic countries.

My final point concerns Glynn's treatment of deterrence and British irresolution, an important issue. One cannot help but ask why the British weren't more forthright, and what the consequences would have been if they had been. As I think he rightly notes, that question has to be directed not only at British policy in the July crisis, but all the way back to the first Moroccan crisis.

Let me make a couple of remarks regarding that point. First of all (and this is a relatively minor remark), my sense of the consensus in historical literature is that even a more forthright British declaration earlier in the July crisis would not have prevented war because the German army was determined to go to war. As a result of the Schlieffen Plan, Germany discounted any British impact on fighting. Indeed, the Schlieffen Plan, as you know, was designed to win the war quickly, precisely because of the coalition that the Germans rightly expected to face. That is to say, in the First World War, the Germans underestimated Britain's impact on the war on the Continent; and in the Second, they overestimated it to their detriment and, I suppose, to our benefit.

Second, although it is true (as Glynn argues) that one reason the British were not more forthright and resolute, one reason they did not practice the policy of deterrence, was domestic divisions, there is another, more controlling reason, an international one. Grey expected to mediate the conflict and saw Britain as the mediator. This expectation is important for our purposes because it bears on a difference between 1914 and our own day.

In 1914, the world was multipolar, the alignments were not clear, and it was reasonable and prudent for the British to behave as they did. Indeed, as you know, from 1912 to 1914 (basically between the end of the Anglo-German naval rivalry and the onset of the July crisis), Anglo-German relations improved quite dramatically. At the same time, Anglo-Russian relations deteriorated. So, had we been sitting around a conference table in Britain in August 1913, talking about where and when the next war would come and who would fight it, I think we all would agree that the likely conflict—if Britain were to become involved—would have been with Russia. Now, that's historical trivia—but of major interest, I think, precisely because this was a multipolar, and not a bipolar, world. The lessons for us of the July crisis, for the central task of deterrence, are not terribly useful.

PATRICK GLYNN: I'd like to respond to Mr. Mandelbaum because his remarks were so thoughtful and detailed and also because they do touch on a critical issue of general interest that we might want to discuss further.

First, since my article is just one chapter of a book, it really doesn't deal with the issue of the change caused by nuclear weapons, which is, of course, dealt with in a different chapter.

But the question immediately arises as to what degree these pre-nuclear historical analogies are valid in the nuclear age. Historically, I think Mandelbaum is incorrect. It's true that today we say with some common agreement that war would be suicidal, unthinkable, and so on. But in fact, the change in thinking about war did not come in 1945—it came in 1919. If you had been talking to a British group in the 1920s, as Stanley Baldwin, Neville Chamberlain, and others did, this kind of statement about the suicidal character of war would have been agreed on without very much quibble by at least most liberal-minded British.

I think that point illustrates that these relationships between changes in technology and changes in politics—and changes in sensibility and changes in strategy—are a lot more slippery than they would appear at first glance. I think that in terms of understanding how we think about war, 1945 is not a significant dividing line, oddly enough. Far more important is 1919, because by 1945 the arguments and strategies were already there. If you read Bernard Brodie on strategic air power, he is essentially recapitulating what people had written about air bombing in the 1930s.

So the issue concerning the degree to which nuclear weapons have changed perceptions and politics is slippery. I think that since the late nineteenth century there has been a kind of Anglo-American ambition to segregate military issues from politics on the grounds that this division seems a reasonable thing to do. It seemed somewhat reasonable before the First World War. It seemed so reasonable after the First World War that the British sought an international convention that would entirely civilianize air power—a little bit like our old ideas for international control of atomic energy.

There was a notion that certain kinds of weapons and strategies could simply be segregated out from political conflict. That, it seems to me, is in itself a projection of the democratic mentality, of the way that democracies deal internally with these kinds of conflicts by segregating power and conflict from other areas of life. The problem is precisely that other regimes and cultures don't share this view. In the Soviet Union in particular there is no basis for it. Gorbachev simply has a new line. They have always had a propaganda line, but if you read the long tradition of Soviet thinking about these issues, you will find that this whole impulse to segregate arms and politics—which I would argue is essentially an alien impulse in politics that has a specific historical origin in classical liberal democracy and in an attitude about military affairs that grew up well before the atomic bomb—is present in democracies. The difficulty with arms control negotiations is that it's not present elsewhere.

The difficulty with nuclear weapons is that, as suicidal and mad as they are, they are effective weapons in the physical sense— too effective in some ways. They are enormously destructive, and they can be used to destroy other weapons. Although they're only held in potential, they always cast a long political shadow. The notion or the ambition to segregate these weapons is not something that becomes more reasonable with the arrival of nuclear weapons. Although the notion may have seemed reasonable in 1929 and 1930, it was only a cultural figment; unless and until other cultures begin to look at nuclear weapons, and thus the world, in a similar way, real arms control is not a possibility. What needs to occur for successful arms control is a fundamental change in the nature of Soviet policy and culture. For this reason, I don't think that nuclear weapons are that important a dividing line for purposes of politics and arms control—except for us. There are some exceptions, because we have a common interest in doing certain things at the margins.

A funny thing about arms control is that people who argue in favor tend to divide into two camps and sometimes switch back and forth. When arms control seems to be politically on the run, people say, "If we don't do this, the world is going to end." Then, when arms control seems to have flaws, they shift ground: "This is really nothing more than a modest tool." It seems to me that there have always been these two views of arms control. My sense is that when we consider, not necessarily the SALT Treaty, but the ABM Treaty, we're talking about a very major change in our strategy, a treaty that cut off a whole variety of technologies that would have changed the configuration of power. The ABM Treaty has been an important inhibition to us. Even in Congress it's an important political inhibition. So I don't discount its importance at all. I think it's a symbolic issue, but symbolic issues often rule politics.

Michael Mandelbaum also raised some historical issues that I'd like to touch on. It seems to me that the argument that the German military was popular is not an argument against the proposition that the German regime was authoritarian. As I spell out in my article, it is precisely in authoritarian cultures that military build-ups and aggressive foreign policy become rallying points. That does not make the culture democratic. In fact, that this kind of issue has resonance makes the culture undemocratic. So the fact that the *Flottenverein* ("Navy Leagues") was the largest public association in Germany is an index of the authoritarian and somewhat atavistic character of the regime. It used old-fashioned peasant control devices of rallying people to nationalism and jingoism as a way of solidifying support for the government.

I'd like to make just one final point about the issue of deterrence. It is definitely arguable, as I try to point out in my article, whether a signal at the beginning of the Sarajevo crisis from the British might have changed the course of events. I think a case can be made for it, but many historians don't believe it; whether the British could have controlled the crisis once it began is debatable. The point is that the framework of deterrence would have been strong had the British opted for a bipolar world, a policy that the Russians, and to some degree the French, were urging on them. As a result, a political structure that would have been a more certain deterrent against German ambitions could have been erected.

W. SCOTT THOMPSON: I can agree with both Pat Glynn and David Singer in the essential thrust of their argument. I do, however, have a problem with Pat Glynn when he goes from being a political animal to a political theorist, and I have the reverse problem with David. What I heard a few minutes ago was an argument I hadn't really heard for twenty years: The issue of political systems theory versus the internal conflicts of the individual, or the single case, was really buried in the 1920s and in the 1960s.

I think we are looking for commonalities. The fact that policy makers are going to make decisions with or without a case study of several thousand instances of conflict is really not terribly meaningful. But there are correlates or commonalities to look for and policy makers later on will be better off for having done so.

Rather than using T.S. Eliot on Shakespeare, I think the better analogy would be to go to a social science that would bring you closer to politics. You might take economics, for example, and you could compare Donald Trump or Lee Iacocca to Paul Volker. You can have Donald Trump if you want him, but it seems to me that a Paul Volker understands the interrelation of theory and action.

So this idea doesn't detract one whit from what Glynn wrote in his article. I would say that the article is a great illustration of the fact that, in Washington, ideas do have power. David's work has shown, and will increasingly show, that we do have something to learn from the building of theory.

ROBIN RANGER: I think Patrick Glynn's work is extremely relevant. The more one can illustrate to policy makers and the public the fact that all the arguments that are currently made about the desirability and feasibility of arms control (both bilateral and multilateral) have all been made before, the better. Many of the problems that we are experiencing in arms control negotiations and agreements reflect a generic problem of the Anglo-American democracies. They are almost always trying to get agreements to limit weapons and almost always find it very difficult to persuade nondemocratic governments to accept these kinds of agreements. Right now, one of the major problems we have with arms control is the Iraqi use of chemical weapons and the failure of the Anglo-American democracies to impose penalties for its use. To the extent that he illuminates the difficulties in multilateral arms control agreements, Glynn's work is especially useful. The Iraqi use of chemical weapons is setting a terrible precedent. Quite frankly, we're fumbling this particular issue, just as the British fumbled the issue of Mussolini's use of chemical weapons in 1935 and 1936. I would also underline the extent to which Glynn is right to stress that the British have beaten a path for misdirections in arms control during the twentieth century.

Now I will switch to a more specific point, which reinforces everything Glynn has said, that historians have had a basic fallacy when they analyze the past: they usually assume that what happened was what had to happen. (This is one of the problems with Paul Kennedy's recent book, *The Rise and Fall of the Great Powers: Economic Change and Military Conflict from 1500 to 2000*.) I think we should ask how we would view the Anglo-German naval competition if Germany had won the war. What if the Schlieffen Plan had worked a little better, maybe not giving the Germans a decisive victory, but improving their naval position by giving them bases on the French coast? What would have happened if the German fleet had then engaged the British fleet, as it could have done, in the first few months of the war? The answer is quite simple: Germany would have won. In the first few months of the war, the German High Seas Fleet was roughly numerically equivalent to the British Grand Fleet, although the British had acquired two extra capital units that were just being completed in Turkey. If the war had broken out a month later, these two units would have been in Turkish hands and used against the British. As a result, the British would have been effectively down four battleships—two sold to Turkey and two detached to watch the Turkish battleships. The result would have been that the British Grand Fleet would have had only eighteen operational capital units in the North Sea (fourteen battleships and four battle cruisers), with four capital units (two battleships and two battle cruisers) in the Mediterranean and two battle cruisers in the Falkland Islands. Against these eighteen British capital units in the North Sea, the Germans could have fielded twenty capital units (sixteen battleships and four battle cruisers). In addition, the German battleships were qualitatively superior to the British fleet because of the way they were built, in accordance with Grand Admiral Tirpitz's risk theory. This is a difficult admission for a former British citizen to have to make, but unfortunately scholarly accuracy compels me to make it.

Thus, the arms race did not bring about World War I; rather, the British failure to compete effectively enough in the arms race very nearly cost the Anglo-French-Russian alliance the war. If the British had been knocked out in 1914, they would not have been able to support the French as they did, and the French would have had to capitulate in turn or to fight a purely defensive campaign to hold on to their remaining territory. So a result would have been the equivalent of the 1917 Brest-Litovsk Treaty (or something even worse) imposed on the Russians by 1915, because there would have been nothing to stop the German armed forces except the Russian forces, and they weren't up to the job. This point is extremely important in terms of how we view the naval arms competition from the viewpoint of arms race theory.

Indeed, if you look at the evidence and then ask—"What if things had turned out a little differently?"—you find out that the Sarajevo interpretation, far from making the case for arms control, really does the reverse. This is certainly true in terms of the naval force programs. You also make the alarming discovery that the major cause of Britain's losing the war was the British failure to compete effectively enough in the naval arms race. You really can document this fact to an extraordinary extent, which reinforces everything else Glynn has said.

RAYMOND L. GARTHOFF: I think Glynn's is a very useful, stimulating article, as has been evident from the discussion. My first point is akin to one Michael Mandelbaum has already mentioned. The Sarajevo fallacy may affect evaluation of that crisis without necessarily being relevant to contemporary concern for accidental war or to arms control in general. I think suggesting such relevance pushes the argument too far.

The new revisionism on the history of July and August 1914 does not necessarily affect other historical or conceivable future cases of less than deliberate, calculated attacks, especially in the nuclear age. Nor does it carry us very far in evaluating arms control, which I think needs to be looked at in terms of the feasibility and the advantages and disadvantages of any particular measure.

War does not necessarily arise from arms races or failures of deterrence. I think more attention ought to be given to the possibilities that war can be stimulated by accident or miscalculated initiation or escalation of hostilities. As far as accidental or incidental measures are concerned, it seems to me that the assassination of Archduke Franz Ferdinand had something to do with Sarajevo and was not instigated by any of the powers.

People make wars by blunders as well as by design. Sometimes they do so because of considerations relating to weapons, whether because of a feeling of strength or a fear of the strength of others or because of the characteristics of particular weapons. It seems to me that the implicit analogy isn't more convincing either in the domestic or in the international sphere.

I think a case can still be made for gun control—for international gun control—although people, rather than guns, kill. Deterrence is only one means of preventing an adversary's attack.

Another way, of course, is to attack him first. Deterrence is also a means of preventing wars, but it is only one of a number of approaches. There are other political and diplomatic means that can be used instead of—or, better still, along with—military means of deterrence.

Finally, I think the question on the nature of regimes may or may not be crucial. I don't think there is any evident correlation, but one needs to study specific cases—specific regimes, democratic or not, and their aims, perceived interests, and threats. I don't think that a case is made that the lesson of history is Munich plus Sarajevo rather than Munich minus Sarajevo. I don't think either equation yields an answer on any particular case with respect to causes of the outbreak of war or the role that arms control can play in preventing it.

I would like to comment very briefly on two specific points. First, I disagree with Glynn: I don't think the Soviets have yet been tested on whether they're ready to give up a first-strike capability. They haven't offered to do so unilaterally. They have at least proposed to do it bilaterally, which we have not. So far both sides have been too conservative and cautious to approach a question of actually giving up all offensive nuclear weapons.

Second, I would simply note disagreement on the question of whether nuclear weapons are important only in our thinking about war. I think they're extremely important in Soviet thinking—perhaps today even more than in the United States. But in any event, I think there is a very wide range of possibilities we need to consider when looking at the ways in which various political and military measures, both unilaterally and through negotiation, can best serve our security interests.

STEVEN MILLER: I found this to be a very stimulating article, and it provokes me to thoughts that are beyond what this discussion will tolerate in terms of length.

Let me enumerate three or four points. I should say in the interest of candor that I come as the default standard bearer of the Sarajevo fallacy, having edited the book that provided Patrick Glynn with some of his major punching bags (*Military Strength and the Origins of the First World War*). I will begin by saying that one of the things I found perplexing, and maybe even disturbing, is that I agree with much of the article and this leads me to my first criticism.

I think Patrick Glynn offers what is a quite common (and, I believe, predominant) interpretation of the origins of the First World War, and he treats it as if it were a tendentious correction of a fundamental misreading. It's simply not true that the authors he attacks ignore Fritz Fischer. In fact, Steven Van Evera, the primary victim of Patrick Glynn's analysis, is the single greatest champion of Fritz Fischer among the younger generation of political scientists. If you look at Van Evera's footnotes, Fritz Fischer appears no less than fifty times. So it is hard to see how that argument stands firm. I should also say as a footnote, since Van Evera's not here to speak for himself, that, as I read through Patrick Glynn's essay quite carefully, time and again I kept saying, "I don't recall this being Van Evera's argument: this seems like a different essay than the one I recall editing." I was so provoked that I reread Van Evera's article, and I think in virtually every instance in which Van Evera is referred to by Glynn, Van Evera's interpretation is closer to Patrick Glynn's than the one that Glynn attributes to him.

Just to give you one example, Glynn suggests that Van Evera doesn't recognize that the true ultimate source of the war was German expansionism; I refer you to the following sentence: "Before 1914 Germany sought a wider sphere of influence or empire and the war grew largely from the political collision between expansion of Germany and resistant Europe." This is completely in accord with Patrick Glynn's interpretation, not 180 degrees away from it: Van Evera agrees with Patrick Glynn on the British; he agrees with Patrick Glynn on the British guarantee to the French; he agrees with Patrick Glynn on the nonessentiality of the Russian mobilization as a cause of war. I think there is a false disagreement here that may serve rhetorical purposes but is an inaccurate representation of Van Evera's views.

I similarly think that the arms race paradigm, which is under assault here and which, in my judgment, deserves most of the assault that it receives, has had its importance and prevalence exaggerated beyond all recognition. Are there people out there who believe the sorts of things that Patrick Glynn describes? Yes. Are there many? No. Are they common in the academic community of people who view these things? Certainly not. Have they dominated the policy community? I believe not at all. Certainly I would say that the views Glynn attacks here are light years from being, "the powerful orthodoxy rarely challenged in the Western foreign policy," as he calls them. I think that is simply wrong. I disagree completely.

With respect to the action-reaction phenomenon (which somehow has become bound up in this whole dispute), it is certainly true that simple action-reaction phenomena do not cause war. I don't know who seriously advocated this position over the past two decades, but to say so is not to repudiate the interactive dynamic between potentially hostile adversaries. Are we to believe that the behavior of one has no impact on the perception and behavior of the other? It seems to me that this is a more preposterous belief than the rest. Of course there's interaction; of course there's action-reaction. In fact, one of the things that bothered Charles Fairbanks is that Glynn's analysis provides a lot of evidence that there was action-reaction in the pre-World War I period, and I think there has been a lot since. In fact, as people have hinted, deterrence depends on this very dynamic; deterrence depends on another state's reacting to our military policy. If we have a world of autistic powers not influenced by our military policy, our military investments, or our military forces, we're in much bigger trouble than if we're really dealing with a hostile power.

I'd like to make two other points. I disagree with the basic proposition that arms control theory derives primarily from World War I or the Sarajevo fallacy. I think it's exactly the reverse. We became interested in World War I because there was interest in arms control. In my view, arms control is driven by concerns about surprise attack in the late 1950s. People were interested in World War I because it looked like an interesting case where surprise attack played a major role. David Singer wrote one of the important books on this subject, and perhaps he can speak on it.

Last, with respect to some of that substantive point having to do with the German expansionists, I think most of us would agree that the Germans were willing to risk war; the Germans were willing to wage war. The problem for them was that they didn't get the war they wanted. Why did they believe expansion was an attractive policy? Because they thought it was going to be profitable. Why did they think it was going to be profitable? Because they believed that they could win it at an acceptable or a reasonable cost. Why did they believe this, in light of the fact that they expected to fight a continental war against a coalition whose actual and potential resources exceeded their own? The answer is that they had a theory of victory just as they did in 1940. They believed in the efficacy and primacy of decisive surprise attack, which meant it was both opportune to strike and also dangerous not to, because decisive surprise attack operated for you; and maybe it operated for your enemy. If you waited, he might strike first.

ANNE CAHN: My remarks are based in part on the comments made this afternoon, as well as on points made in Patrick Glynn's article. Several previous commentators have pointed out that the article takes a static view of the world. If we haven't changed our military thinking since 1945, then we are in deep trouble. Nuclear weapons are not just bigger and better conventional weapons. Historically, the more weapons you had, the better off you were, because all those weapons had potential for political use. I believe that nuclear weapons have no acknowledged political use what-soever. If one side has 11,324 nuclear weapons and the other side has 10,184, it really doesn't make one iota of difference. I think the political uselessness of nuclear weapons is a new phenomenon that has not existed before.

Also, I think there are new phenomena taking place, phenomena that are not static. The discussions going on right now between the military leaders of the Soviet Union and the military leaders of the United States are simply unprecedented. What these generals and admirals are asking each other is this: "What is it about my forces that you find threatening? What bothers you the most?" I think these kinds of discussions are going to lead to new kinds of bilateral and multilateral arms control discussions and negotiations and new ways of thinking about such negotiations.

Glynn also spoke about the huge superstructure of arms control. I think it's worth pointing out that the entire budget for the Arms Control and Disarmament Agency is something on the order of $30 million a year, compared to $300 billion a year for the Defense Department. I think this disparity translates to about one penny for arms control for every $100 for defense, so I'm not sure where this huge superstructure of arms control really is.

What I want to learn from Glynn is: What's the bottom line of his article? Is it that all arms control is bad? That arms control is detrimental to our national security? That we're worse off because we have an agreement, or would we be worse off yet if we had a START agreement? I'm not quite sure that I understand what the point of the article is.

LUCJA U. SWIATKOWSKI: I agree with what Glynn said in his article, but I have to join others in the criticism that the article is somewhat unidimensional and that we must look at the broader conflicts of politics and culture.

I think that what Robin Ranger said about the Anglo-Saxon nature of this whole debate holds true; the reason is not because the United States and Britain were more democratic than other countries, but because other countries felt that their just political demands could not be satisfied within the prevailing international political system. Michael Mandelbaum said that the competition between great powers over colonies in 1914 certainly constituted one dimension of the war. In addition to this competition, there was a tension between the great powers and the subject peoples, not only in the Third World but also in Eastern Europe. It was only as a result of World War I that East European nations regained their national independence. The Third World countries basically had their independence demands satisfied after World War II.

There is also, within these societies, a demand for political and economic equality, which becomes evident in the latter half of the nineteenth century. Dr. Glynn mentions in his article that the

Germans diverted internal equality struggles into external forums. That is an important dimension that requires more discussion.

Thus the issue of peace and disarmament involves not only technical issues of deterrence and arms control, but also political issues of justice in relations between and within states. The concept of what is just changes over time. In modern times, there is a certain consensus that national independence, or at least cultural autonomy, and political equality are reasonable demands that ought to be satisfied.

As a result of World War I, these demands were satisfied in Eastern Europe. Even though the Eastern Europeans despised the destruction that war brought them, which was probably the greatest, they still regarded the outcome—the Versailles Treaty that brought them independence—as good. Glynn mentions in his article that as a result of World War I, the British pursued disarmament and an appeasement policy in the interwar period. However, when we look at Eastern Europe that was not the outcome at all. Practically, British actions meant that they were sympathetic to German demands for the revision of the Versailles Treaty, which ultimately threatened the independence of the Eastern European states. The result was the German attack on Czechoslovakia and Poland and World War II. Thus disarmament is not a value in itself but derives its meaning from its political context. In this particular context, disarmament meant war, not peace.

The concept of war as an arbiter of last resort in resolution of political conflicts obviously played an important role in the past, but it is basically unacceptable in the age of nuclear war. Everybody agrees that a nuclear war is neither acceptable nor desirable. In this respect, I believe it has already been mentioned that arms control does not deal with significant political conflicts but with marginal issues. Therefore, to resolve international conflicts and accommodate the new demands for political and social justice evident in the world today, we need a flexible international political mechanism to respond to those demands; and we do not have it today.

One last, brief point about the nature of democratic regimes: Colonel Summers raised the issue of whether, in democratic countries, the public really has the influence over foreign affairs and operative issues of war and peace that we assume it has. If it does have a moderating influence, then the main demand we should make of the Soviet Union is not for arms control, but for democracy in the Soviet Union and Eastern Europe. That would make the world a much more peaceful place.

MARK BLITZ: My tendency is to agree with the importance of basic political motivations as central, but I'll fight that tendency a little bit.

First, the practical intentions of countries are shaped in a subtle way. I think that the intentions of any country in situations similar to that of Germany (circa World War I) are to some degree shaped by what other countries have proved themselves capable of and by a government's perception of whether other countries are indeed as capable as they pretend.

In practice, the question here would be this: Who deserves an empire, anyway, and why don't we deserve one? There's a sense in which your shaping of your intentions (and your conception of your possibilities) is very much connected to what others have done and to the new situations brought about by what they have done. Similarly, I think that your conception of your own practical intentions is shaped by the tools you have available. These are not simply a matter of your discretion or, to some degree, of anybody's. There are technological tools that were not previously available, which can give a practical reality to your intentions and give you some thoughts that you might not otherwise have had. So, practical situations can in this sense come into being apart from a simple, easy statement of basic political intention.

The second broad point I want to make deals with the question of political regimes. To have an adequate sense of the question of whether democracies are more or less prone to be aggressive, one first has to look carefully at the question of how democracies or republican regimes relate to each other. The classical Kantian notion is that somehow they are not aggressors in relation to each other. To really think this whole issue through, one also has to come to grips with the notion of democratic imperialism. It can't simply be the case (and hasn't been the case) that countries defined as democratic regimes are never aggressive. Rather, one must concentrate on their relation to each other and then look at the way a country shapes its practical intentions in relation to its notion of what it deserves vis-à-vis what others are already holding or are capable of holding.

So perhaps there is a bit more to what's behind some versions of the view Glynn argues against, although the truth is basically on his side.

HARRY G. SUMMERS, JR.: I want to make just one remark from a military point of view regarding the point made earlier with respect to nuclear weapons. From my experience teaching at the Army War College for the last six years, I must say that nuclear weapons have had a profound effect on strategy: since 1950, the United States military has been on a strategic defensive. It has fought two wars on the strategic defensive, in Korea and in Vietnam, both with profound implications of what the military can do on a battlefield. Essentially, the strategic defensive means that you cannot win decisively on the battlefield: the best result obtainable is stalemate, and the only way to end a war is through diplomatic rather than military means. This profound limitation on the use of military forces comes directly from the limiting factor of nuclear weapons. So if it is true that war has changed fundamentally in response to nuclear weapons, this change can be summarized in the three rules of strategy: don't march on Moscow, don't march on Moscow, and don't march on Moscow. That certainly has been the case; we're not going to march on Moscow as long as they have nuclear weapons. But, conversely, they're not going to march on Washington either.

There has been a fundamental strategic change in concepts of fighting. The nuclear threshold has become a major limiting factor. Just to close the whole question of arms control and the Intermediate Nuclear Forces (INF) Treaty—to really understand INF—one has to realize that for the military, intermediate nuclear forces had no military utility. So to give them up meant giving up nothing. The reason why INF was so easy to obtain on both sides was that the treaty gave away weapons systems that had no real value from a military viewpoint.

CHARLES FAIRBANKS, JR.:   I want to take up a point that was brought up by David Singer, Michael Mandelbaum, and Steven Miller, that is, the question of how important the World War I case—the Sarajevo case—is for contemporary policy. I think this question is crucial: Is the World War I/Sarajevo case important or not? I take the side that it's very important.

Let me specifically comment on Dr. Singer's suggestion that we need to look at the more than one thousand cases of conflict since 1850. I agree. But we have to make a distinction between the source of the evidence and the source of the hypothesis that we're testing. The source of the evidence has to be all those conflicts, even the ones before 1850, as much evidence as we can intelligently gather and assimilate. (Thucydides described the arms race between Corcyra and Corinth, for example.) But the hypothesis that arms races cause wars has a specific historical origin. In those thousands of years that there were arms races, not one was ever called an *arms race* until 1893.

Before then, no action-reaction mechanism is attributed to these competitions. It's not said that they caused a war. What I would say to David Singer is that the hypothesis that he's been testing comes from the period of World War I. It seems to me that a real reproach to the field of conflict studies is that it does not know where its central hypothesis and central concept come from. They can be determined only by historical study. As a matter of fact, if you read enough from the nineteenth century, you'll find out where that concept came from and why people started believing in it when they never believed in it before.

Does World War I have much to teach us or not? I'm not sure how much the actual process of the causation of war in 1914 has to teach us. I'm sort of agnostic or unsure about that point. I think it can teach us where our own beliefs come from, because they do come from that period, without any question, and I think it's a great achievement of Patrick Glynn to see that.

J. DAVID SINGER: Charles Fairbanks's last comment is intriguing, and I'll start by rejoining. First of all, I don't use the phrase *arms race*. I talk about arms rivalry, and we have very operational criteria as to what constitutes an arms rivalry. We've got to pay much more attention to the sources of our hypotheses because often they can contaminate the way in which you define a research problem and form any results.

We've done what I think is a fairly compelling statistical study, and there is no statistically significant difference between the propensity of autocratic or democratic regimes either to get into wars or to initiate wars. I very much appreciated what I heard from Mark Blitz on that point. The comment that we keep hearing (as seen on bumper stickers) is "Guns don't kill, people kill." I always say that's an absolutely useful statement. The fact is that you can't fight wars without people and weapons, thus recalling the suggestion made by people like Morgenthau and Kennan back in the 1950s, that a nation is only armed when it perceives a threat to its security and that the threat to its security will begin to disappear as the arms disappear. We have much historical evidence, as well as logical evidence, to make us skeptical about such statements.

One of the things that struck me in Glynn's comments has to do with the implication that only the Soviets have deployed first-strike weapons. I think we must make very clear the incredible symmetry in the propensity of certain powers to deploy weapons systems that have a lot of first-strike characteristics. I certainly don't want to suggest that any weapon system is one or the other. All weapon systems, both qualitative and quantitative, have both a deterrent and a provocative effect. What we need to do is maximize the deterrence to provocation ratio.

Glynn also suggested that the kind of research I'm doing isn't very helpful to the policy process. The implication is that we don't start doing research until we're in the middle of a crisis! The whole idea of doing research in medicine or social-systems engineering is to try to generate knowledge and to produce findings so that as the crises appear on the horizon we don't have to start calling Michigan, Harvard, Stanford, and MIT to ask, "What do we do now?" Looking at medical diagnoses and medical treatment, people are beginning to make machine readable, storable, and accessible what we know from medical research, so that when a physician comes on a new case or new crisis he or she can say,

"Here's what we found out: eighty-seven percent of the time when you have this syndrome the correct diagnosis was this rather than that."

One other point I would like to do has to do with accidental war. There's no such thing. Every war is the consequence of a mix of intentional and unintentional results. Some of us may find war undesirable. Some of us may find a particular war unexpected, but *some* will expect it. Some will *desire* it. Hard-wiring the northern hemisphere with the kind of weapon systems we have today is equivalent to taking a hotel building, putting a five-gallon can of high-octane gasoline in every room with a fuse out into every corridor, and giving everybody, as he or she leaves the bar, a lighter. How, then, can we say that when the hotel blows up, it was an accident? The notion of accidental war is a very dangerous, misleading, and perhaps dishonest one.

Finally, the notion that some states are more prone to wage war or more eager or receptive to war—and to treat that as dichotomous—is very misleading. Every state has a set of national security elites who cluster around these positions. That not only varies from one section to the other in each nation, but also varies across time. To suggest that it is the inherent aggressiveness of one state and the inherent acceptability of war—even Charles Fairbanks was making a comment suggesting that the Russians are afraid of what we will do when we find out what is really on their minds—you're giving aid and comfort to those who believe the funny hypothesis that the Soviets are really committed to world domination.

ROZANNE L. RIDGWAY: As a practitioner, I look around this table of scholars and appreciate very much the invitation to join them and the opportunity to read the Glynn article in preparation for today. I believe that this very important article gives an academic surrounding to a point of view, which in today's bureaucracy needs an academic surrounding.

One point of view is obvious around this table. It has much academic support and is probably the popular one on campus and in academic writings. It's about time that somebody on the other side began to address the question of arms control.

Having said that, I must say that almost everything else that I've heard—including the last statement about national security leaders clustering around war propensities—makes me conclude that there's almost a total lack of connection (and, indeed, I fear a dysfunctional lack of connection) between this world of scholarship and scholars and the world of those of us who are negotiating arms control with the understanding that it is simply one of several instruments of national security policy. Arms control in the U.S.-Soviet relationship is the principal topic behind this discussion. It tends to be European in scope. I suspect, with the discussion of nuclear weapons, that in the area of arms control, one does not find the central issues of the U.S.-Soviet relationship or, indeed, the question of how countries go to war. That question is not found in the area of arms control. That's all I want to say. I appreciate what's driving this discussion today, but I'm having trouble admiring the attempt (and indeed a very successful one) to put some scholarship to the question of why one needs to be leery of agreements on arms control.

There's not much between this world and mine today. I end up where Anne Cahn did, asking what the bottom line of all this is.

MICHAEL MANDELBAUM: I have two points. First, I said arms control has been a marginal enterprise. Patrick Glynn quite rightly called me on that by mentioning the ABM Treaty, which was not marginal. That treaty, however, goes to one of the central issues we've been discussing: whether nuclear weapons have changed the world. If nuclear weapons have not changed the world, then the ABM Treaty makes no sense: it's certainly not in the interest of the United States. Of course, some people think it is; I do. The point is that those who think so, a group that apparently at one point included most of the political community in the United States, think on the basis of a judgment that nuclear weapons are different from all others and have changed military strategy fundamentally.

The second point concerns the one real area of difference between Patrick Glynn and me and, I think, between me and Charles Fairbanks—or between Steve Miller and me, on one side, and Glynn and Fairbanks on the other. I certainly don't deny the existence of a certain mindset, an outlook on international affairs that Glynn has correctly characterized as the Sarajevo fallacy. He has described it well: it does have a history, and indeed goes back before World War I. It probably even goes back to Cobden and Bright but got an enormous boost from World War I.

That view—that cluster of attitudes—was wrong about how the world worked before 1945. Even if one concludes that nuclear weapons have changed the world, the Sarajevo fallacy mindset cannot be entirely appropriate for our own time. But because people believe it, it ought to be discussed, it ought to be contended with, and it ought to be criticized when it deserves criticism. What I don't believe is that it has had any significant impact on policy even in the liberal Anglo-American countries where it has been most predominant.

Now the Sarajevo fallacy viewpoint becomes a historical argument, but let me give it to you cryptically. First, I think these ideas were important for British policy in the 1920s, not the 1930s. The Liberal government of 1905, which Glynn discusses, was a repository of some of the ideas. Nobody can go back and read about that government without being struck by the resonance with ideas of our day. There are people in the so-called Economist factions saying Britain shouldn't be spending this much on defense, that it ought to negotiate more, that arms are dangerous. All true. Some of that sort of thinking existed. Yet even in the Liberal party, I believe even in the Economist factions that preferred butter to guns, there was always a consensus in favor of two propositions. One was that Britain had to maintain naval superiority over Germany—although there was a lot of interest in trying to do so by negotiation. Note *superiority*, not *parity*. The second was that Britain could not accept the deal that the Germans were offering, that is, stopping the naval rivalry in return for a free hand on the Continent. Such a deal would have undercut one of the two pillars of British strategy, which was to make sure there was never a dominant power on the Continent. So a consensus existed even among those who harbored these ideas in favor of a foreign policy that defended Britain's basic interests. That is perhaps an esoteric case.

If we take that kind of argument and apply it to the present situation, in the post-World War II United States, there has been and continues to be consistent consensus on various policies in favor of (1) containment of the Soviet Union in Europe and (2) nuclear deterrence. Those are the core policies of the United States on which deterrence and the American position in the world depend. Those core policies decide war and peace, and the United States has pursued them, notwithstanding the facts that liberal ideas do get a hearing and do have a constituency here and that this is a democracy.

JOHN NORTON MOORE: I think this has been a very provocative and informative discussion. I have just one comment on the substance and then a couple of methodological questions. First, in addition to asking about the origins of World War I, it is also interesting to address the question of the origins of U.S. involvement in World War I. This somewhat different issue may, I suspect, also illustrate Patrick Glynn's thesis of deterrence failure from a different perspective.

If deterrence failure was indeed a major problem leading to World War I, presumably that failure resulted not from a lack of power on the part of the British, but from a failure of communication. A clear strategy of deterrence means working with others to send clear signals that war would be futile.

Although I'm not a historian of this period, I gather that the U.S. involvement in World War I was almost a flip of deterrence failure. President Woodrow Wilson indicated to the Germans that a continuation of the policy of attacking American merchant shipping would bring the United States into the war. The Germans made a deliberate decision to continue—indeed, to escalate—because of a calculation that it would take the United States more than a year to be effective in the war. In that one year, if the Germans could make unrestricted attacks against merchant shipping, they would be able to prevail before the United States could enter the war.

So, in essence, it was a deterrence failure (if it was one) from the opposite role of deterrence theory; that is, not a failure to send clear signals, but a failure to have the necessary ability to back those signals with something that the other side would take seriously in the overall equation. I would urge Glynn to look at this somewhat separate issue of U.S. involvement in World War I in addition to the outbreak of World War I itself.

To proceed to the methodological comment and question, it seems to me that as Glynn continues his work, it will be sharpened if he differentiates more clearly the range of different kinds of questions that he addresses.

One of the difficulties for the audience and commentators in what was an extremely interesting, provocative, and important article is that many of the different questions we're addressing today could each be the subject of a book or a discussion of its own. Here are some examples: arms races as a factor in causing war; deterrence failure as a factor in causing war; the extent to which these are elements in World War I; the effect of any Sarajevo fallacy on policy, and the shift at that point to arms control itself. Other questions to consider are these: What lessons, if any, does one learn about arms control or its effect either on deterring or enhancing (modestly) the risk of war? What are the implications for democracies in the use of arms control? What kinds of unique opportunities or problems (or perhaps both) are there as democracies seek to deal with this task and many others? In short, one of the potent sources of intellectual confusion that we always have in this kind of setting is that there are many different issues, each worthy of careful examination. My point is not, in any sense, to question the overall value of the generalized discussion we've had but merely to plea for rigorous care in posing the full range of issues as Dr. Glynn's work proceeds.

My last methodological point is that Scott Thompson is correct in noting that we need not choose between believing that generalization is important for human thought and believing that drawing an analogy from a variety of circumstances is inherently impossible. Trying to look at serious empirical approaches and to obtain as much useful data as we can is, of course, frequently helpful. Things are true or false in the real world because they are, not because they're supported by either one generalization or 120 (although if we have 120 generalizations, it may tell us something more about the degree of confidence that we would have in the particular assessment).

This last point is one that prompts me to leave some questions with this distinguished group. We don't have time to answer them today, but I would be grateful for any letters or comments because we're really trying to deal with these issues at the United States Institute of Peace. What is the state of human knowledge in this field? What can we do to try to enhance it? What kinds of empirical studies might be useful? How should those empirical studies be conducted? Where can empirical work be usable and where is it to date giving only pseudo-knowledge?

In this area the questions have been asked poorly. As a result, we're getting poor answers. Let me give you a few examples. I happen to be a proponent of good empirical research, and so I offer some examples of the things I've seen in the literature that strike me as possibly leading only to pseudo-knowledge, comparable to telling us that coffee keeps us awake because it contains a wake-ative agent. Take statistics that show great likelihood of conflict where there tends to have been an arms race or a greater arms build-up on all sides: Do those statistics really tell us anything? Is this viewpoint useful, or isn't it almost a self-fulfilling prophecy? One side aggressively seeking to wage war is presumably engaging in a military build-up as part of that design, and others frequently build in response.

That example simply illustrates the question of whether some statistical information is really useful. Let me suggest one last example of statistical information—one that's troubled me in the literature that looks empirically at the role of certain political systems and their relationship to the use of force. I refer to the counting technique of suggesting that the attack by Germany on Poland counts as one for Poland, just as it counts as one for Germany. That is, the use of force score is one for Nazi Germany and one for Poland. Now it seems to me that if we are proceeding in this way—including settings such as the U.S. deployment to the Persian Gulf with the Nazi invasion of Poland—then we're obviously ending up with pseudo-knowledge that may, indeed, be harmful to our real understanding of the issues.

PATRICK GLYNN: This has been an extremely useful discussion. Both the people who agreed and those who disagreed said useful things, and their ideas will help me sharpen my thinking as I move on in my work. So, I am grateful.

There has been a tension in discussion between bumper-sticker assertions about policy and the more sophisticated, scholarly statements that one can make about these phenomena. I wouldn't want anyone to get the impression that I believe, for example, that nuclear weapons didn't change anything in 1945. My point is simply that the possibility of segregating military issues from political issues is no greater in the presence of nuclear weapons. I have a lot to say about what the changes were, but I'm not going to bore you with that now.

I want to get into two substantive issues. One is the importance of the Sarajevo fallacy, because this is an issue that Steven Miller and Michael Mandelbaum both raised in different ways. As I read the political scene and the policy scene, the Sarajevo fallacy is very much alive and well and very much a part of discussion of policy to people who are writing important books. When I gave my article to Owen Harries at the *National Interest*, he had just read a new book by Bill Hyland, which had a long passage on the importance of the First World War in studying nuclear arms control and superpower relations. Kissinger's memoirs, which came out in the 1980s, devoted a long passage, part of which I quoted, to this. The notion that this somehow had been discovered—that it was common knowledge, that Fischer was accepted and so on in the policy community—from my reading, is just wrong. The fallacy is still out there, and I think that there are many, many people who would still be surprised by my article.

I did not state in my article that Van Evera had not read Fischer. In fact, the striking thing about the Van Evera article, and that volume in general—the thing that really surprised me about it—is that this was a group of scholars who had read Fischer and who had still come to a variation of the same conclusions that the earlier revisionists had reached. That struck me as remarkable.

I think this variation was similarly apparent in the tension in Steven Miller's remarks. On the one hand, he said, "This is something we all know," but on the other hand, he disagreed with me on substance. Well, that's precisely my quarrel with Van Evera and the passages that I quoted. Van Evera takes this issue and then says that, well, of course, we know Germany was responsible, but the real underlying cause of the war was the cult of the offensive, a certain kind of military strategy that was current at the time. This seems to me another form of saying, "Well, it's arms races, it's these general things, that cause wars." In proposing a solution, he proceeds in much the same way: that is, he argues that a more conciliatory approach by Britain, more open communication in the international environment, and an eschewing of offensive strategies would have been the way to circumvent the conflict.

It seems to me that on a higher, more sophisticated level, Van Evera is saying fundamentally the same kinds of things that people who have depended upon the revisionist paradigm have said all along; namely, that if everybody were less offensive, we could negotiate, share principles, and avoid conflicts like World War I. So it seemed to me Van Evera and others swallowed and digested Fischer without his theory having had any effect on their thinking about policy. That's one reason, I suspect, that many people read that volume without coming to a new consensus. That's why there weren't ripples, why you could pick up a book by Bill Hyland several years later and see the same fallacy repeated.

Finally, I will turn to one interesting historical point made by Michael Mandelbaum, a point where I think we do disagree. I agree, generally speaking, with his characterization of the Economists' outlook, the outlook of the Economist faction of the Liberal party, but I would point out that this is as true of national security liberals today. That didn't mean there weren't important practical differences on policy. One of them, discussed in my article, was the disagreement over how to respond to the intelligence scare of 1909. In fact, yes, Economists like Churchill believed in naval superiority, but their underlying preference was for a smaller navy. This led them to read intelligence estimates in such a way as to make arguments for less British response to Germany, rather than more. I would argue that fundamentally the same thing has happened in our national security community: that there is a group that will acknowledge very realistically that these are problems, but in practical instance after practical instance, when there's a judgment call (as there often is), they tend to come down on the side of less and less. The difficulty with this approach is that it was precisely the mixed policy pursued by Grey—that is, the kind of half-hawk, half-dove policy that made British deterrence strategy inefficacious at the time. It's precisely these mixed policies that democracies pursue as a compromise, as it were, between common sense and the Sarajevo fallacy that can get us into trouble, because they present an ambiguous face to an opponent and can be exploited. So while we agree in substance, I still think, in practice, there was a difference there.

Again, I want to thank you. In addition to being a very useful endeavor for peace research, this discussion was very useful for me. I want to thank those with whom I don't take issue, like Mark Blitz and Lucja Swiatkowski, who attempted to get at some of the more subtle oversimplifications that one necessarily engages in when writing an article of this length on this subject.

Appendix

DR. MARK BLITZ joined the Hudson Institute in Indianapolis as Senior Research Fellow and Director of Political and Social Studies in January 1989. Previously, Dr. Blitz was Associate Director of the United States Information Agency. Educated at Harvard University and the University of Pennsylvania's Wharton School, Dr. Blitz taught at the University of Pennsylvania, Harvard University, and Georgetown University. He has been Assistant Director of ACTION, Director of the Office of Private Sector Programs at the United States Information Agency, and the Senior Professional Staff Member of the Senate Committee on Foreign Relations. Dr. Blitz has published books and articles on political philosophy as well as foreign relations.

DR. ANNE CAHN is Senior MacArthur Scholar at the Center for Strategic Studies, University of Maryland. Educated at the University of California, Berkeley, and the Massachusetts Institute of Technology (MIT), Dr. Cahn taught and researched at MIT before assuming a fellowship position in Harvard University's Center for Science and International Affairs, where her work concentrated on arms transfers and nuclear proliferation. She later served as Chief of the Social Impact Staff at the U.S. Arms Control and Disarmament Agency, and then as Special Assistant in the Office of the Assistant Secretary of Defense for International Economic and Technology Affairs. Dr. Cahn currently serves on several boards of directors, including that of the *Bulletin of Atomic Scientists* and the National Security Archive.

DR. ALBERTO COLL is Professor of Strategy and International Law and occupies the Charles H. Stockton Chair of International Law at the U.S.

Naval War College. Educated at Princeton University and the University of Virginia in Law and Political Science, he has also taught at Georgetown University. Dr. Coll has published a number of books and articles in the areas of international politics, law, and organization, national security affairs, Latin America, and the Soviet Union. He is the Editor/Rapporteur for the United States Institute of Peace Project on Strengthening World Order and the United Nations Charter System Against Secret Warfare and Low-Intensity Conflict.

DR. CHARLES FAIRBANKS, JR. is currently Director of the Foreign Policy Institute's Program in Soviet and American National Security and a Research Professor at the Johns Hopkins School of Advanced International Studies (SAIS). Educated at Yale University, Cornell University, and the University of Chicago, Dr. Fairbanks has taught at SAIS, Yale University, and the University of Toronto and has been a Fellow at the Woodrow Wilson International Center for Scholars, the American Enterprise Institute, and SAIS. He has also been Deputy Assistant Secretary of State for Human Rights and Humanitarian Affairs and a member of the State Department's Policy Planning Staff. Dr. Fairbanks has published extensively on a wide range of topics, including Soviet politics, arms control, arms races, national security policy, and Middle Eastern politics. Awaiting publication is his book *Arms Races: from the Dreadnought to SDI*.

MS. DEVON GAFFNEY joined the Smith Richardson Foundation as Foreign Policy Program Officer in 1984. She has served for the last three years as Director of Research, supervising the foreign and domestic policy programs. Prior to her arrival at Smith Richardson, she was Associate Editor of the *Washington Quarterly*. Her experience in Washington included a stint as an editor at *Foreign Policy* and a year as a Research Assistant in the Woodrow Wilson Center's International Security Studies Program. She holds a B.A. from Bryn Mawr College and pursued national security studies at Johns Hopkins School of Advanced International Studies.

DR. RAYMOND L. GARTHOFF is a Senior Fellow at the Brookings Institution. A Foreign Service veteran, he served variously as Counselor of the U.S. Mission to NATO; Deputy Director of the Bureau of Politico-Military Affairs, Department of State; Executive Officer and Senior Advisor on the U.S. SALT Delegation; Senior Foreign Service Inspector; and Ambassador to Bulgaria. Dr. Garthoff has written on national security and Soviet political and military affairs, including *Detente and Confrontation: American-Soviet Relations from Nixon to Reagan* (1985), *Soviet Military Policy* (1966), and *Soviet Strategy in the Nuclear Age* (1958).

DR. PATRICK GLYNN is a Resident Scholar at the American Enterprise Institute, where he is currently completing a book on the history of arms control entitled, *Closing Pandora's Box*. From 1986 to 1987, he served as Special Assistant to the Director of the Arms Control and Disarmament Agency. Educated at Harvard University, Dr. Glynn has served as Coeditor of the *Journal of Contemporary Studies*, and his articles have appeared in *Commentary*, the *New Republic*, and the *National Interest*. Dr. Glynn's article, "The Sarajevo Fallacy: The Historical and Intellectual Origins of Arms Control Theology" (*National Interest*, Fall 1987) was the subject of this Public Workshop.

AMBASSADOR OWEN HARRIES is Coeditor of the *National Interest*. Educated at the Universities of Wales and Oxford, Ambassador Harries held various academic appointments in Australia before serving as the Senior Advisor to Australian Prime Minister Malcolm Fraser and as head of Policy Planning in the Department of Foreign Affairs in Canberra. From 1982 to 1983, he was Australia's Ambassador to UNESCO. Ambassador Harries has contributed numerous articles to scholarly journals and is the editor and principal author of *Australia and the Third World*.

DR. KENNETH M. JENSEN is Director of Research and Studies at the United States Institute of Peace, where he was previously Director of the Grants Program. Dr. Jensen holds degrees in History, Russian, and Soviet Studies from the University of Colorado, University of Wisconsin, and Moscow State University, USSR. His doctoral research and subsequent scholarship has focused on Russian Marxist social and political thought. He is the author of *Beyond Marx and Mach* and numerous articles, papers, and reviews in the Russian and Soviet field and is consulting editor of *Studies in Soviet Thought*. Dr. Jensen is also editor (with Fred E. Baumann) of three recently published books on American policy issues: *American Defense Policy and Liberal Democracy; Crime and Punishment: Issues in Criminal Justice;* and *Religion and Politics*.

AMBASSADOR SAMUEL W. LEWIS became President of the United States Institute of Peace on November 1, 1987, after thirty-one years as a Foreign Service Officer. He retired from the State Department in 1985. In his last post, he was United States Ambassador to Israel for eight years, first appointed by President Carter and then reaffirmed by President Reagan. He was a prominent actor in Arab-Israeli negotiations, including the Camp David Conference, the Egyptian-Israeli Peace Treaty, and U.S. efforts to bring the Israeli invasion of Lebanon to a peaceful conclusion. He had previously served as Assistant Secretary of State for International Organization Affairs, Deputy Director of the Policy Planning Staff, Senior

Staff member on the National Security Council, a member of the United States Agency for International Development mission to Brazil, Special Assistant to the Under Secretary of State, and in lengthy assignments to Brazil, Italy, and Afghanistan. Before coming to the Institute, Ambassador Lewis was Diplomat-in-Residence at the Johns Hopkins Foreign Policy Institute and a Guest Scholar at the Brookings Institution. He is a graduate of Yale University (*magna cum laude*), earned an M.A. degree in International Relations from the Johns Hopkins University, and also spent one year as a Visiting Fellow at Princeton University.

DR. MICHAEL MANDELBAUM is currently a Senior Fellow at the Council on Foreign Relations and is the Director of its Project on East-West Relations. Educated at Yale, Cambridge, and Harvard universities, he taught and researched at Harvard and Columbia universities for a number of years. Dr. Mandelbaum has also been Research and Editorial Director of the Lehrman Institute and has served in the Office of the Undersecretary for Political Affairs, U.S. Department of State. A well-known expert on nuclear issues, Dr. Mandelbaum is the author of *The Fate of Nations: The Search for National Security in the 19th and 20th Centuries*.

DR. STEVEN MILLER is currently conducting research at the Stockholm International Peace Research Institute (SIPRI) in Sweden. Prior to his position at SIPRI, Dr. Miller was an Assistant Professor of Political Science and Research Associate in the Defense and Arms Control Studies Program at the Massachusetts Institute of Technology's Center for International Studies. He was also Coeditor of *International Security* and an Adjunct Research Fellow at the Center for Science and International Affairs, Harvard University. Dr. Miller is the author or editor of numerous publications on foreign policy, nuclear weapons, and security, including *Military Strategy and the Origins of the First World War* and the forthcoming *Nuclear Arguments: The Major Debates on Strategic Nuclear Weapons and Arms Control*.

PROFESSOR JOHN NORTON MOORE was appointed by President Reagan to be the first Chairman of the Board of Directors of the United States Institute of Peace. He is the Walter L. Brown Professor of Law and Director of the Graduate Law Program at the University of Virginia School of Law. Professor Moore is also the Director of the Centers for Oceans Law and Policy and Law and National Security. Professor Moore has been Counselor on International Law to the Department of State; United States Ambassador to the Third United Nations Conference on the Law of the Sea; Deputy Special Representative of the President to the Law of the Sea Conference; Chairman of the National Security Council Interagency Task Force; and Special Counsel for the United States, arguing two cases before the International Court of Justice. He is the author or editor of numerous books on international conflict management, including *Law and the Indo-China War, Law and Civil War in the Modern World,* and *The Arab-Israeli Conflict.*

MR. CHARLES E. NELSON is Vice President of the United States Institute of Peace. Before joining the Institute, he served as Vice President of an American export trading company doing business with Latin America. Previously he worked with the RAND Corporation as an executive in its housing and civil justice programs, which included an emphasis on dispute resolution. He has also worked with the Agency for International Development and a private consulting firm on economic and social development in the Middle East, Africa, and Latin America. He is a graduate of Harvard College, Harvard Law School, and the National War College.

DR. ROBIN RANGER is currently a Peace Fellow in the Jennings Randolph Program for International Peace at the United States Institute of Peace. His fellowship project is entitled "Compliance Policy: The Key to Reducing International Conflict Via U.S.-Soviet Arms Control Agreements." Educated at the London School of Economics, he has been a lecturer and professor at universities in Canada, the United States, and Great Britain. Dr. Ranger has published widely on the history and problems of arms control, including his 1979 book *Arms and Politics 1958–1978: Arms Control in a Changing Political Context.*

AMBASSADOR ROZANNE L. RIDGWAY was Assistant Secretary of State for European and Canadian Affairs from 1985 until 1989. A native of St. Paul, Minnesota, and graduate of Hamline University, her Foreign Service career has taken her to Manila, Palermo, Oslo, Nassau, Helsinki, and Berlin. Ambassador Ridgway's assignments in Washington have concerned educational exchange, NATO political affairs, U.S.-Ecuadorian relations, Latin American policy planning and coordination, and special bilateral negotiations while attached to the Office of the Secretary of State. Ambassador Ridgway achieved ambassadorial rank in February 1976 when she was confirmed as Ambassador for Oceans and Fisheries Affairs. In September 1989, Ambassador Ridgway succeeded Mr. George M. Seignious II as President of the Atlantic Council of the United States.

DR. J. DAVID SINGER has been Professor of Political Science at the University of Michigan, Ann Arbor, for the past twenty-three years. Educated at Duke and New York universities, Dr. Singer has also taught at colleges and universities in the Netherlands, Switzerland, and West Germany as well as at Harvard University, Vassar College, and the U.S. Naval War College. He has published widely and is perhaps best-known for his *Correlates of War* study. His selected papers are soon to be published. Familiar to the United States Institute of Peace, Dr. Singer served on the Jennings Randolph Review Panel and was a colloquium participant in the Intellectual Map Project.

COLONEL (RET.) HARRY G. SUMMERS, JR. is Editor of *Vietnam Magazine*, Contributing Editor for *U.S. News & World Report*, and a syndicated columnist. He formerly held the General Douglas MacArthur Chair of Military Research at the U.S. Army War College. Twice decorated for his valor on the battlefield and twice wounded in action, Colonel Summers is a combat infantry veteran of the Korean and Vietnam wars. His book based on the Vietnam experience, *On Strategy*, is used as a student text by all the armed forces' war and staff colleges and by many civilian universities. Awarded a B.S. in Military Science by the University of Maryland in 1957, Colonel Summers also holds the degree of Master of Military Arts and Sciences from the Army Command and General Staff College.

DR. LUCJA U. SWIATKOWSKI, a native of Warsaw, Poland, attended Columbia University School of Engineering and graduated from Barnard College. She holds Master of Philosophy and doctorate degrees in International Relations and Soviet and East European studies from Columbia University where she also attended the Russian Institute and the International Fellows Program. Dr. Swiatkowski's doctoral dissertation, "The Imported Communist Revolution and Civil War in Poland, 1944–1947," is under contract with Oxford University Press. In 1985–1986, she was a Guest Scholar at the Brookings Institution, and she has worked as a consultant to Radio Free Europe and the Office of Technology Assessment. In 1987–1988, Dr. Swiatkowski was the Director of Soviet Studies at the National Institute of Public Policy. Currently a consultant at the World Bank, she is conducting a major study on the Council of Mutual Economic Assistance. She is coauthor of a group study *Crisis Stability and Nuclear War* (1988) that evaluates the performance of command systems of all nuclear powers during international crises.

DR. W. SCOTT THOMPSON serves on the Board of Directors of the United States Institute of Peace. Dr. Thompson is Professor of International Politics at the Fletcher School of Law and Diplomacy, Tufts University. A Rhodes scholar and a graduate of Stanford and Oxford universities, Dr. Thompson has been White House Fellow, Assistant to the Secretary of Defense, and Associate Director of the United States Information Agency.

He is the author or editor of numerous books and articles on foreign policy; is a founding member of the Board of the Committee on the Present Danger; is a member of the Council on Foreign Relations and the International Institute for Strategic Studies; and serves on the Board of the Institute for Strategic Trade. He is currently on sabbatical from the Fletcher School and is spending the year at the Carnegie Endowment for International Peace.

MR. LEON WIESELTIER is Literary Editor of the *New Republic*. He was educated at Columbia, Oxford and Harvard universities. Prior to assuming his present position, he was a member of the Society of Fellows at Harvard, during which time he studied Jewish history and literature. His articles on literary, Jewish, and political subjects have appeared in numerous newspapers and journals, including the *New York Review of Books, Commentary, Dissent,* and the *American Scholar*. Mr. Wieseltier's book *Nuclear War, Nuclear Peace* has been widely acclaimed. He also serves as Contributing Editor of *Partisan Review* and is a member of the Council on Foreign Relations.

The Research and Studies Program

To complement its research grants and fellowships for organizations and individuals, the United States Institute of Peace established its own Research and Studies Program in 1988.

Research and Studies projects are designed and directed by the Institute, which supervises their implementation with the assistance of expert consultants and/or contract researchers. Most projects are carried out through a process which includes the production of working papers on a selected topic and their discussion by experts in public session. Proceedings from the sessions are redrafted as papers, reports, articles, monographs, and books to assist scholars, educators, journalists, policymakers, and citizens' groups in understanding issues of peace and war.

Research and Studies activities fall into four main categories: study groups, public workshops, working-group projects, and studies. Study Group projects run from 4–6 months and involve a core group of expert participants in intensive examination of near-term international conflict situations. Public workshops are two- to three-hour events designed for group discussions around a discrete topic of current concern. Working-group projects run for one year or longer and proceed through four or more public sessions involving a core group of expert participants. Studies are conceived on the same scale as working groups, but with a changing cast of participants. In all of these activities, the Institute strives to provide representation of a wide range of points of view, and to address its mandate to contribute to and disseminate knowledge about ways of achieving peace by doing as much work as possible in public session.

Kenneth M. Jensen
Director

Acknowledgments

The editors wish to thank Editorial Assistant Lilly J. Goren and Project Officer David Wurmser for their editorial assistance in preparing the manuscript for this publication. They also wish to express their appreciation to Aileen C. Hefferren for her editorial advice and production assistance, to Joan Engelhardt for production management, and to Marie Marr-Williams for manuscript tracking.